D1399048

QUALITY
Quality Sports
COACHES

NATIONAL STANDARDS
FOR ATHLETIC COACHES

RICHARD W. NORTON
MEMORIAL LIBRARY
Louisiana College
Pineville, Louisiana

National Association for Sport and Physical Education

Copyright © 1995 by the
National Association for Sport and Physical Education
(NASPE)

ISBN 0-7872-1282-2

All rights reserved. No part of this publication may be reproduced,
stored in a retrieval system, or transmitted, in any form or by any
means, electronic, mechanical, photocopying, recording, or otherwise,
without the prior written permission of the copyright owner.

Printed in the United States of America
10   9   8   7   6   5   4   3   2   1

Table of Contents

796.077
N277

138206

National Association for
Sports and Physical Education

Sport Task Force

Vern Seefeldt, Director, Youth Sport Institute, Michigan State University

Jack Acree, Athletic Director, Boise City Schools

Jody Brylinski, Professor of Physical Education, Western Michigan University

David Feigley, Director, Youth Sports Research Council, Rutgers University

Pat Sullivan, Professor of Physical Education, George Washington University

Brent Steuerwald, Director of Physical Education and Athletics, Shenendehowa Central School District, New York

Staff
Tim Rose, Program Administrator

Judith C. Young, Executive Director

Acknowledgements

The National Association for Sport and Physical Education extends special thanks to the Youth Sport Institute of Michigan State University under the direction of Dr. Vern Seefeldt for the extensive review of existing research on coaching and coaching programs. Dr. Michael Clark also made significant technical contributions to the development and revision of the various drafts of the documents.

Special thanks are also extended to the Sporting Goods Manufacturers Association for financial contributions to this project.

National Standards for Athletic Coaches

Background

The **National Standards for Athletic Coaches** are the result of a consensus project facilitated by the National Association for Sport and Physical Education (NASPE), an association of the American Alliance for Health, Physical Education, Recreation and Dance (AAHPERD). For more than 30 years, NASPE, in collaboration with the National Association for Girls and Women in Sport (NAGWS), has been advocating quality coaching and coaching education. We have published "Guidelines for Children's Sports," position statements on "Coaching Certification," "Guidelines for Coaching Education: Youth Sports," as well as Handbook *for Youth Sport Coaches* and *Parent's Complete Guide to Youth Sports*. Many other organizations have collaborated on many of these projects. A special task force was appointed by the NASPE Cabinet in 1992. One of the charges to this task force was to consider ways to improve the quality of coaching, building on all previous initiatives. Using research assistance from the Youth Sport Institute at Michigan State University, an extensive review of all coaching materials took place. This review included material from National Sport Governing Bodies (NGBs), youth organization programs, college university programs, American Sport Education Program (ASEP), Program for Athletic Coaches Education (PACE), Canadian Coaching Program, research on coaching, role delineation studies, etc. Based on this review, a draft document was developed, outlining what coaches should know and be able to do, as a basis for expanding discussion among many individuals with interest and experience in coaching at various levels. This document was the focus of extensive discussion and input at a National Coaching Summit held in March, 1994 and hosted by the U.S. Sports Academy. Over 200 organizations and other individual experts were invited to participate in the Summit. Representatives of these organizations came together for two and a half days of discussion centered on the draft of the standards. A new draft relecting input from all participants was prepared and sent to all those invited to or attending the Summit and others who requested information about the standards. More than 600 copies have been distributed for input. Presentations about the standards have been made at major meetings including AAHPERD (state, district and national levels), the Commission on Sports Medicine and Science, the American Academy of Pediatrics (AAP), the National Alliance of Youth Sports (NAYS), and the American College of Sports Medicine (ACSM). Further revisions were incorporated based on additional feedback from coaches, athletic directors, youth sport administrators, the legal profession, etc.

Purpose

The **National Standards for Athletic Coaches** are intended to provide direction for administrators, coaches, athletes and the public regarding the skills and knowledge that coaches should possess. These standards reflect the fundamental competencies that administrators, athletes and the public should expect of athletic coaches at various levels of experience. Unprecedented expansion of the information that is available to coaches requires a higher standard of care regarding the health and safety of athletes. Coaches, because of their primary roles as teachers and mentors of athletes, must aspire to and achieve high standards and have resources available to assist them in gaining needed skills and knowledge.

The **National Standards** are viewed as a means whereby additional individuals—especially women and minorities—will be encouraged to enter the ranks of coaches. Rather than be exclusive, these competencies should encourage individuals, particularly at the volunteer level, to aspire to the qualifications that are appropriate for coaching athletes at various levels of achievement. Directors of programs should view these standards as an effective way to evaluate the sports experiences of athletes. Adoption and achievement of the standards should lead to increased opportunities for coaches and athletes alike.

These competencies also provide increased opportunities for persons within the framework of the Americans With Disabilities Act. Although the full impact of the law on the implementation of athletic programs is not clear, an increased commitment to include athletes and coaches with disabilities is embedded in these competencies. While the needs of athletes with disabilities may be met most effectively by coaches, administrators and trainers who have specialized competencies, the pervasive theme in these standards is for coaches to provide for the maximum participation of all athletes in a supportive, reassuring and safe environment. The standards were also developed with an awareness that individuals with disabilities can and should be effective coaches.

Finally, these standards and competencies are viewed as part of a dynamic compilation of the knowledge, skills and values that are associated with the effective and appropriate coaching of athletes. New information will demand that The standards be reviewed and updated on a regular basis. **The overriding premise in the development of this document is that its contents be used to ensure the enjoyment, safety and positive skill development of America's athletes.**

Description of Coaching Levels

The 37 standards are grouped in eight domains and appropriate competencies are identified to further define and delineate the meaning of each standard. The eight domains are as follows:
- Injuries: Prevention, Care and Management
- Risk Management
- Growth, Development and Learning
- Training, Conditioning and Nutrition
- Social/Psychological Aspects of Coaching
- Skills, Tactics and Strategies
- Teaching and Administration
- Professional Preparation and Development

In order to provide a progression of qualification, the competencies associated with the standards were divided into five levels with each domain represented at each level.

Level one is intended to represent a minimum entry level qualification for any individual who begins to coach. The remaining levels represent a model for designating increasing levels of expertise in coaching. The mastery of all standards and the associated competencies defines the fully competent master coach.

What the Standards are Not

It is not intended that the **National Standards for Athletic Coaches** be a certification program or be the basis of a single national assessment for all coaches. The Standards are put forth to help organizations and agencies who currently certify coaches, provide coach education/training, evaluate select coaches, or design programs to meet the needs of perspective and practicing coaches. Also, the standards are not sport specific. Therefore, it will *continue* to be the role/responsibility of all sport sponsoring organizations to develop appropriate sport and situation specific programs using the **National Standards for Athletic Coaches** as a basis or framework for design of selection, evaluation and education programs.

How to Use This Document

How to Use This Document

Domains, Standards and Competencies

The following document represents 37 standards in five levels covering 8 domains of knowledge and ability. The standards are further delineated by approximately 320 competencies. Collectively these standards and competencies represent the **National Standards for Athletic Coaches.** These standards and competencies appear in three formats. The first format lists the standards **as components of the eight domains**. The second format for the standards is a description **by level**; the standards are described within each of the 5 levels so that the reader is able to see which competencies are suggested at each coaching level. The third version provides the competencies **in a matrix**, by level and domain. In this format only the numerical and letter designations of the competencies are listed.

In describing the individual competencies, the reader will see that the competencies are reflected in the coach, in progressive degrees as coaching levels increase; the progression is as follows: Awareness, Application, Mastery, Internalization. Consider the following examples from the domain, *Injuries: Prevention, Care and Management*: At Level 1, Standard 1, competency a—*recognizing the environmental and safety hazards*—should be mastered and internalized by all coaches. However, 1g—*knowing that safety equipment, coach's vigilance and other safeguards provide protection*—should be an "*Awareness*" at Level 2 and "*Mastered*" at Level 3. In other words, coaches should understand the importance of the topic at Level 2, but they will not be expected to have full command of the concept until completing Level 3. However, once a topic has been identified at "*Mastery*," it will continue as a coaching competency for all subsequent levels.

Other designations refer to expansion of awareness or application, which suggest that coaches can apply the information to decision-making or coaching practices. *These* distinctions are based upon the topics themselves. "*Application*" applies to factual information or acts to be accomplished, such as in *standard 4g—using medical information forms for collecting essential medical data*. Generally, "*Internalizaion*" is used in reference to skills or attitudes that should be part of the ongoing professional development of coaches. Examples include *know how to recognize and respond to symptoms of injuries or know when professional medical care is required,* which are *standards* 6e and 6j. However, some topics must be continually renewed and updated after *Mastery* if they are particularly important. In such instances, repeated review and application allows coaches to gain *Mastery* and ultimately *Internalization*, suggesting that coaches should reconsider them as often as possible.

Rationale for the Levels

The approximately 320 competencies within the eight domains represent a comprehensive, but not necessarily exhaustive, list of qualifications that coaches at the respective levels should possess. In order to provide a hierarchy or progression of qualifications, the competencies are divided into five levels, with each domain represented at each level.

Level 1 represents minimal standards for a beginning coach. The remaining four levels are provided here as models. However, sport and coaching organizations may develop alternative levels in a manner suitable to specific programs of coaching development. The task force on coaching standards realizes that coaching selection, evaluation and development programs must fit the requirements of various governing bodies, state high school athletic associations and volunteer youth coaches organizations. Some organizations that currently require certain standards of qualifications for coaches may find that these standards suggest an upgrading or an increase in their current criteria or requirements for education.

The suggested experience associated with each level is as follows:

Level 1   These competencies should be acquired of all coaches prior to the time they conduct a practice or direct their athletes in a contest. Several of these competencies reflect the need for Level 1 coaches to receive continual guidance in working with athletes.

Level 2   These competencies are pertinent to beginning sports coaches who have had at least one season of experience.

Level 3   This level corresponds to the entry level competencies expected of a coach at the interscholastic level. Coaches who teach more highly skilled athletes at whatever age, and those who coach select or elite youth athletes should have acquired these competencies.

Level 4   These competencies describe the knowledge, skills and values to be attained by experienced, professional coaches who have more than one full season of experience at an interscholastic or equivalent level or who teach highly skilled athletes at whatever age.

Level 5   These competencies describe the highly experienced master coach who functions at the highest levels of amateur, interscholastic, intercollegiate, national or international levels. Additional qualifications or competencies will likely be required by sponsoring organizations.

Although the levels are identified as representing increasing expertise of coaches, typically the standards and competencies in Levels 1 and 2 should be reflected by volunteer coaches of beginning to intermediate athletes (usually children and youth). Scholastic coaches should typically meet standards at Level 3 and higher. Finally, coaches of elite and collegiate athletes should meet standards at Levels 4 and 5. However, coaching competency is not a function of the athletes that are coached. Hence, for example, a master coach (Level 5) may coach beginning athletes.

Considering the diverse situations faced by coaches at these five levels, only the most common elements of coaching have been included; thus, this list represents the **essential competencies** to be possessed by coaches who function at each of the five levels. To deal with the specialized needs of competitors at the upper levels, the administrators responsible for selecting these coaches should consider the requirement of additional, specialized qualifications, depending on the needs of the athletes involved. Thus, the emphasis of this document is on the basic knowledge required of coaches at each level as they progress from a novice to a highly skilled professional, master coach.

National Standards for Athletic Coaches

Listing of Domains and Standards

National Standards for Athletic Coaches

Domains and Standards

Domain: Injuries: Prevention, Care and Management

Standard 1.   Prevent injuries by recognizing and insisting on safe playing conditions.

Standard 2.   Ensure that protective equipment is in good condition, fits properly and is worn as prescribed by the manufacturer; ensure that equipment and facilities meet required standards [American Society for Testing Materials, (ASTM) and U.S. Consumer Product Safety Commission, (USCPSC)].

Standard 3.   Recognize that proper conditioning and good health are vital to the prevention of athletic injuries.

Standard 4.   Prevent exposure to the risk of injuries by considering the effects of environmental conditions on the circulatory and respiratory systems when planning and scheduling practices and contests and implementing programs for physical conditioning.

Standard 5.   Be able to plan, coordinate and implement procedures for appropriate emergency care.

Standard 6.   Demonstrate skill in the prevention, recognition and evaluation of injuries and the ability to assist athletes with the recovery/rehabilitation from injuries that are generally associated with participation in athletics in accordance with guidelines provided by qualified medical personnel.

Standard 7.   Facilitate a unified medical program of prevention, care and management of injuries by coordinating the roles and actions of the coach and a National Athletic Trainers Association certified athletic trainer with those of the physician.

Standard 8.   Provide coaching assistants, athletes and parents/guardians with education about injury prevention, injury reporting and sources of medical care.

Domain: Risk Management

Standard 9.   Understand the scope of legal responsibilities that comes with assuming a coaching position, *i.e.* proper supervision, planning and instruction, matching participants, safety, first aid and risk management.

Standard 10.   Properly inform coaching assistants, parent/guardians and athletes of the inherent risks associated with sport so that decisions about participation can be made with informed consent.

Standard 11.   Know and convey the need and availability of appropriate medical insurance.

Standard 12.   Participate in continuing education regarding rules changes, improvements in equipment, philosophical changes, improved techniques and other information in order to enhance the safety and success of the athlete.

Domain: Growth, Development and Learning

Standard 13.   Recognize the developmental physical changes that occur as athletes move from youth through adulthood and know how these changes influence the sequential learning and performance of motor skills in a specific sport.

Standard 14.   Understand the social and emotional development of the athletes being coached, know how to recognize problems related to this development and know where to refer them for appropriate assistance when necessary.

Standard 15.   Analyze human performance in terms of developmental information and individual body structure.

Standard 16.   Provide instruction to develop sport-specific motor skills. Refer athletes to appropriate counsel as needed.

Standard 17.   Provide learning experiences appropriate to the growth and development of the age group coached.

Domain: Training, Conditioning and Nutrition

Standard 18.   Demonstrate a basic knowledge of physiological systems and their responses to training and conditioning.

Standard 19.   Design programs of training and conditioning that properly incorporate the mechanics of movement and sound physiological principles taking into account each individual's ability and medical history, avoiding contraindicated exercises and activities and guarding against the possibility of over-training; be able to modify programs as needed.

Standard 20.   Demonstrate knowledge of proper nutrition and educate athletes about the effects of nutrition upon health and physical performance.

Standard 21.   Demonstrate knowledge of the use and abuse of drugs and promote sound chemical health.

Domain: Social/psychological Aspects of Coaching

Standard 22.   Subscribe to a philosophy that acknowledges the role of athletics in developing the complete person.

Standard 23.   Identify and interpret to co-coaches, athletes, concerned others and the general public the values that are to be developed from participation in sports programs.

Standard 24.   Identify and apply ethical conduct in sport by maintaining emotional control and demonstrating respect for athletes, officials and other coaches.

Standard 25.   Demonstrate effective motivational skills and provide positive, appropriate feedback.

Standard 26.   Conduct practices and competitions to enhance the physical, social and emotional growth of athletes.

Standard 27. Be sufficiently familiar with the basic principles of goal setting to motivate athletes toward immediate and long range goals.

Standard 28. Treat each athlete as an individual while recognizing the dynamic relationship of personality and socio-cultural variables such as gender, race and socio-economic differences.

Standard 29. Identify desirable behaviors (i.e. self discipline, support of teammates, following directions, etc.) and structure experiences to develop such behaviors in each athlete.

Domain: Skills, Tactics and Strategies

Standard 30. Identify and apply specific competitive tactics and strategies appropriate for the age and skill levels involved.

Standard 31. Organize and implement materials for scouting, planning practices and analysis of games.

Standard 32. Understand and enforce the rules and regulations of appropriate bodies that govern sport and education.

Standard 33. Organize, conduct and evaluate practice sessions with regard to established program goals that are appropriate for different stages of the season.

Domain: Teaching and Administration

Standard 34. Know the key elements of sport principles and technical skills as well as the various teaching methods that can be used to introduce and refine them.

Standard 35. Demonstrate objective and effective procedures for the evaluation and selection of personnel involved in the athletic program and for periodic program reviews.

Domain: Professional Preparation and Development

Standard 36. Demonstrate organizational and administrative efficiency in implementing sports programs, *e.g.* event management, budgetary procedures, facility maintenance, participation in public relations activities.

Standard 37. Acquire sufficient practical field experience and supervision in the essential coaching areas to ensure an adequate level of coaching competence for the level of athlete coached. This would include a variety of knowledge, skills and experiences.

National Standards for Athletic Coaches

Complete with Competencies

National Standards for Athletic Coaches

Domains, Standards and Competencies

Indicated after each competency is the level at which mastery or achievement is expected

Domain: Injuries: Prevention, Care and Management

Standard 1. Prevent injuries by recognizing and insisting on safe playing conditions.

a. Recognize the environmental and safety hazards likely to affect athletes in practice and competition—such as wet or slippery surfaces, structures in or near activity areas with which athletes may collide, such as walls, fences and goals standards, sprinkler heads or spectator seating—*Level 1*

b. Establish and follow procedures for identifying and correcting unsafe conditions—*Level 1*

c. Stop or modify practice or play when unsafe conditions exist—*Level 1*

d. Ensure that qualified individuals are present to officiate all competitions—*Level 1*

e. Require the use of appropriate and adequate safety equipment by all athletes during practice and competition—*Level 1*

f. Know and apply the rules and policies related to the safety and welfare of athletes in the sport being coached during all practices and competition—*Level 1*

g. Know that safety equipment, coach's vigilance and other safeguards provide protection against injury to athletes—*Level 3*

h. Be active at your level of coaching in working for the formulation of rules that influence the safety and healthful participation of athletes in the sport coached—*Level 4*

Standard 2. Ensure that protective equipment is in good condition, fits properly and is worn as prescribed by the manufacturer; ensure that equipment and facilities meet required standards (ASTM and USCPSC).

a. Know what safety equipment and facilities are needed by athletes and required by rules governing competition in the sport coached or otherwise needed for athletic protection—*Level 1*

b. Assist athletes in choosing, fitting and maintaining equipment—including safety gear—*Level 1*

c. Know which items of equipment are subject to recognized safety standards (ASTM, USCPSC) and ensure that all items meet these standards—*Level 2*

d. Know applicable safety standards for the sport coached; regularly inspect all facilities apparel and equipment to assure compliance with all safety requirements—*Level 2*

Standard 3. Recognize that proper conditioning and good health are vital to the prevention of athletic injuries.

a. Instruct athletes in aerobic and anaerobic conditioning programs appropriate for the sport and athletes being coached—*Level 3*

b. Use conditioning drills and activities consistent with the needs of the sport and athlete—*Level 1*

c. Know how aerobic and anaerobic energy is produced and relate these two energy systems to the demands of the sport coached—*Level 3*

d. Prepare practice plans incorporating conditioning activities designed to develop both anaerobic and aerobic energy fitness as required by the sport; indicate which system is being developed—*Level 3*

e. Know the role played by the musculo/skeletal system in skill development and prevention of injuries—*Level 2*

f. Prepare a season coaching plan that indicates when and how conditioning will take place—*Level 3*

g. Understand and be able to implement the different types of muscular training (interval, circuit and weight training) as they relate to sport and athletes being coached—*Level 3*

h. Know how skill instruction, conditioning, preventive care and coaching decisions influence the risk of injury to athletes—*Level 3*

i. Plan in-season and out-of-season activities designed to develop those elements of total conditioning required by the sport—*Level 3*

j. Instruct athletes about off-season programs that will assist in maintaining appropriate levels of general fitness for sport—*Level 4*

Standard 4. Prevent exposure to the risk of injuries by considering the effects of environmental conditions on the circulatory and respiratory systems when planning and scheduling practices and contests and implementing programs for physical conditioning.

a. Be able to describe the functioning of the circulatory and respiratory systems and how these functions react to serious stresses—*Level 3*

b. Recognize the differences of athlete response to circulatory/respiratory stress—*Level 4*

c. Know how such environmental factors as temperature, humidity, altitude and general climate can represent a risk to athletes and how such risk can be reduced—*Level 3*

d. Know how clothing worn for practice and competition can affect the risks associated with various environmental conditions—*Level 3*

e. Prepare practice plans that allow for dealing with dangerous environmental factors; be prepared to limit activity to reduce risk—*Level 3*

f. Provide for unlimited fluid/water intake during physical activity andinstruct athletes about proper hydration and acclamitization—*Level 2*

g. Know the most common pre-existing conditions of athletes, e.g. asthma, allergies, diabetes, improper body fat levels, nutritional deficiencies, cardiac conditions, seizures, repeated concussion, serious orthopedic injury; how to identify those athletes suffering from these conditions; the circumstances in which these conditions put the athlete at unusual risk; how to modify activity to effectively reduce that risk; how to recognize smptoms indicating that the condition is causing the athlete to suffer activity related injury/illness; and how to appropriately respond to such indications—*Level 3*

Standard 5. Be able to plan, coordinate and implement procedures for appropriate emergency care.

a. Know the details of and be prepared to execute the established emergency plan for the organization/activity/situation—*Level 1*

b. Have available a written emergency plan for all sites where practices and competitions occur—*Level 2*

c. Maintain appropriate medical records for each athlete—including medical information or physical examination forms and medical treatment consent forms—*Level 1*

d. Assure that medical information and treatment consent forms are available during all practices and competition—*Level 1*

Standard 6. Demonstrate skill in the prevention, recognition and evaluation of injuries and the ability to assist athletes with the recovery/rehabilitation from injuries that are generally associated with participation in athletics in accordance with guidelines provided by qualified medical personnel.

Prevention

a. Recognize the physical risks in the sport to be coached and how injuries may be prevented or minimized and the importance of reporting all symptoms immediately—*Level 1*

b. Prepare practice plans that indicate where and when dangerous situations may arise and tell how these situations are to be managed—*Level 2*

c. Teach athletes to distinguish among different types of injuries and related pain (for example, sharp pain in joints that may indicate injuries that will worsen if proper rest or treatment are not provided as compared to aches within muscles which may be an acceptable element of conditioning and fitness)— *Level 4*

Care

d. Have knowledge of first aid and CPR, or have immediate access to someone who is first aid/CPR qualified—*Level 1*

e. Know how to recognize and respond to symptoms of injuries that may occur in the sport coached— *Level 1*

f. Have a first aid kit available at all practices and games; know its contents and their appropriate use; know the location of the nearest telephone—*Level 1*

g. Know and be able to apply standard management procedures designed to minimize exposure to blood-borne pathogens (BBPs); know and follow specific contest rules intended to limit exposure of athletes and officials to blood or bodily fluids—*Level 1*

h. Know when professional medical care is required for an injured athlete— *Level 1*

i. Complete and file an injury report form for each medical emergency— *Level 1*

Management

j. Follow guidelines and instructions provided by a NATA certified athletic trainer, team physician and/or other qualified sports medicine professionals in implementation of procedures for returning athletes to play following injury or illness, including when the athlete can resume activity—*Level 2*

k. Consider such factors as the type of injury, the need for reconditioning and the athlete's skill level when preparing a plan for aiding an athlete in returning from injury—*Level 4*

l. Help athletes understand how injury and subsequent recovery programs may affect their level of performance—*Level 4*

m. Require injured athletes to follow through with a conditioning regimen prepared by medical personnel—*Level 4*

n. Teach athletes that rehabilitation of injuries should be initiated under the guidance of medical personnel—*Level 5*

o. Understand the psychological consequences of injury and assist athletes in dealing with them—*Level 4*

p. Help athletes realize how such issues as "playing with pain" influence decisions about recovery programs and the time allotted to them—*Level 5*

q. Allow athletes the time to recover fully from injury before returning to play—*Level 1*

r. Emphasize to athletes that such elements as communication with care givers and skills for coping with becoming dependent upon medical personnel are part of the recovery program—*Level 5*

Standard 7. Facilitate a unified medical program of prevention, care and management of injuries by coordinating the roles and actions of the coach and a NATA certified athletic trainer with those of the physician.

Prevention

a. Consult with a NATA certified athletic trainer or physician for assistance in understanding the physical needs of athletes—*Level 2*

b. Change coaching techniques when a trainer or physician brings the need to do so to the coach's attention—*Level 2*

c. Involve a NATA certified athletic trainer, exercise physiologist or physician of sports medicine in preparing a plan for conditioning athletes for specific sports—*Level 4*

d. Cooperate with qualified medical personnel to prepare a summary of season injuries and analyze the summary of season injuries to discover possible injury patterns—*Level 3*

e. Change coaching techniques and/or conditioning programs when injury patterns suggest a need to do so; for example, if ankle sprains were common, consider whether and how the joint can be made less susceptible through training—*Level 3*

Care

f. Assure that an athlete is referred to a NATA Certified athletic trainer, team physician or other qualified provider upon sustaining an injury which requires more than minor first aid care, and that the athlete does not return to activity without clearance from such provider(s)—*Level 2*

Management

g. Keep a record of communications with health-care providers concerned with the treatment of injured athletes—*Level 2*

Standard 8. Provide coaching assistants, athletes and parents/guardians with education about injury prevention, injury reporting and sources of medical care.

a. Be informed about the availability of clinics, workshops, journals, books and related resources that provide current information about injury prevention, treatment and care—*Level 3*

b. Know sources of information that can be shared with assistant coaches and parent/guardians concerning the care and treatment of injured athletes—*Level 3*

c. Encourage assistant coaches and parent/guardians to participate in educational programs that emphasize the prevention, reporting and care of injuries—*Level 3*

d. Become involved in formulating, publicizing, interpreting and teaching policies and procedures for safe and healthful athletic participation—*Level 4*

Domain: Risk Management

Standard 9. Understand the scope of legal responsibilities that comes with assuming a coaching position, e. g. proper supervision, planning and instruction, matching participants, safety, first aid and risk management.

a. Follow safety guidelines, procedures and risk management plans established by program administrators—*Level 1*

b. In accordance with established administrative procedures and based upon relevant legal requirements, organize and maintain appropriate records as evidence in the event of legal challenges.

Records should include assignments of personnel; practice plans; special safety measures; attendance of athletes; emergency plans;, safety rules/procedures; reports of injuries; copies of records of all oral and written communications concerning an injury or other unusual event)—*Level 1*

c. Provide proper general and specific supervision of athletes—*Level 1*

d. Inspect facilities and equipment for potential safety hazards prior to each use—*Level 1*

e. Know the coaches responsibilities in first aid, CPR and emergency procedures—*Level 1*

f. Know the legal responsibilities of the coach in teaching, supervision, transportation, medical care and communication and how to meet them—*Level 1*

g. Be able to match participants in terms of such characteristics as age, maturity, size, skill and experience; group participants appropriately—*Level 3*

h. Cooperate with administrators and medical providers in developing and regularly reviewing a formal risk management plan—*Level 2*

Standard 10. Properly inform coaching assistants, parent/guardians and athletes of the inherent risks associated with sport so that decisions about participation can be made with informed consent.

a. Know the specific risks to participants and how to reduce these risks for the sport coached—*Level 1*

b. Inform those involved about the risks of athletics by instructing athletes and others concerned about the purpose of agreements to participate and informed consent, medical information, medical release and medical emergency forms—*Level 1*

c. Prior to participation, require the completion of all necessary agreements and medical forms by athletes and guardians—*Level 2*

d. For coaches and participants, conduct and document meetings regarding procedures for safety and emergency and guidelines for risk management—*Level 2*

Standard 11. Know and convey the need and availability of appropriate medical insurance.

a. Distribute information to assistant coaches, athletes and parent/guardians concerned about sources for personal health and liability insurance—*Level 2*

b. Discuss the importance of adequate health and accident insurance coverage with athletes and parents/guardians prior to participation and as needed at other times—*Level 1*

c. Comply with existing requirements regarding insurance for athletic participation and record evidence that all participants have such coverage—*Level 1*

Standard 12. Participate in continuing education regarding rules changes, improvements in equipment, philosophical changes, better techniques and other information in order to enhance the health, safety and success of the athlete.

a. Attend rules meetings offered by appropriate sanctioning groups in order to be informed of rules changes and interpretations—*Level 1*

b. Attend clinics, workshops and/or in-service education programs designed for coaches in order to obtain information necessary for coaching—*Level 3*

c. Read professional publications dealing with the sport coached for information on safety, proper equipment and coaching strategies—*Level 3*

d. When opportunities arise, communicate with other coaches about the sport, how it should be taught and how it can be made safer—*Level 3*

e. Document formal and informal education as evidence of accumulated competence—*Level 1*

Domain: Growth, Development and Learning

Standard 13. Recognize the developmental physical changes that occur as athletes move from youth through adulthood and know how these changes influence the sequential learning and performance of motor skills in a specific sport.

a. Demonstrate knowledge of the general developmental sequence in mental, motor and physical abilities—*Level 4, Level 5*

b. Recognize the physical and motor limitations of athletes common to the age and skill level being coached and adjust expectations accordingly—*Level 3*

c. Choose drills and practice plans which allow athletes the opportunity to improve while not forcing them to extend themselves beyond their physical and mental-emotional limits—*Level 3*

d. Teach skills and strategies that are within the performance limits of the athletes—*Level 3*

e. Recognize the developmental stages of athletes and know how they relate to *a specific* sport as either limits *to* or prerequisites for performance—*Level 4*

Standard 14. Understand the social and emotional development of the athletes being coached, know how to recognize problems related to this development and know where to refer them for appropriate assistance when necessary.

a. Recognize the typical behaviors exhibited by athletes of the age groups being coached—*Level 3*

b. Know the different general stages of social and emotional development of the athletes being coached and realize the developmental differences that may exist—*Level 3*

c. Be aware of social-psychological issues that may affect athletes of different ages in contemporary society; these may include such factors as peer pressure, lowered self-esteem, single-parent families, substance abuse, violence, sexual identity, emotional stress and child abuse—*Level 3*

d. Know how to recognize psycho-social distress and the resources available to assist athletes—*Level 4*

e. Refer athletes with social and emotional problems to appropriate professionals for assistance —*Level 4*

f. Know and educate athletes and parent/guardian how social psychological problems may increase susceptibility to injuries or influence recovery—*Level 4*

Standard 15. Analyze human performance in terms of developmental information and individual body structure.

a. Assess the capabilities of athletes based on age, matureity, size, skill level and experience—*Level 2*

b. Assess athlete success in learning skills relative to their physical limits—*Level 1*

c. Develop practice plans that allow for all athletes to learn new skills at their own pace and within their own limits—*Level 2*

d. Recognize that athlete performance is determined by developmental level, chronological age, experience and genetic endowment—*Level 3*

e. Recognize differences in body structures specific to the age group and sport being coached—*Level 4, Level 5*

f. Know the basic movement capabilities and limitations of various body parts—*Level 4, Level 5*

g. Know the limitations on physical performance of the various elements involved in the body movement—*Level 4, Level 5*

h. Understand the essentials of anatomy and biomechanics as they relate to physical activity generally and specifically—*Level 4, Level 5*

i. Understand how biomechanical factors can limit motor performance skills—*Level 5*

j. Establish performance goals that reflect the developmental levels of the athletes—*Level 5*

k. Know how the body type of athletes affects their performance of the needed motor skills—*Level 5*

l. Know that athletes may extend the limits of their abilities by learning to compensate for specific limitations—*Level 5*

m. Evaluate athletic performance based on possible bodily movements and mechanical limitations of the individual athlete—*Level 3*

n. Prepare season-end evaluations of athlete progress relative to developmental level and relevant variables in body structure—*Level 3*

o. Know which body systems and physiological factors are key to athletic performance, and apply this knowledge in designing training and practices—*Level 4*

Standard 16. Provide instruction to develop sport-specific motor skills. Refer athletes to appropriate counsel as needed.

a.   Recognize the general developmental characteristics of the relevant athlete population and their common problems; these may include such items as problems with eye-hand coordination, visual training needs, growth spurts, maturational problems and over-use injuries—*Level 4*

b.   Emphasize life-long activity and enjoyment of physical activity as goals of athletic participation—*Level 3*

c.   Know community and medical resources are available to assist with problems affecting the athletes coached—*Level 4*

d.   Refer athletes with developmental motor problems for appropriate professional assistance—*Level 2*

e.   Know how such factors as motivation, physical development and emotional maturity influence the ability of athletes to learn new skills—*Level 4*

f.   Aid athletes in assessing their own abilities accurately —*Level 4*

g.   Know the over-all requirements and opportunities of the relevant sport so that athletes can be made aware of opportunities open to them—*Level 4*

h.   Find additional opportunities in the sport for those participants who are highly motivated or particularly capable of higher levels of achievement—*Level 4*

Standard 17. Provide learning experiences appropriate to the growth and development of the age group coached.

a.   Acquire or prepare season objectives that reflect the physical and mental development and levels of the athletes—*Level 3*

b.   Select specific drills and activities that allow athletes of various levels to experience success—*Level 3*

c.   Use a variety of activities to help athletes of various levels of ability develop specific skills—*Level 4*

Domain: Training, Conditioning and Nutrition

Standard 18. Demonstrate a basic knowledge of physiological systems and their responses to training and conditioning.

a.   Know the five essentials of conditioning: Warm up/cool down, overload, progression, specificity and reversibility; implement them according to the developmental level of the athletes—*Level 3*

b.   Know the components of the physiological systems involved with athletic conditioning—*Level 3*

c.   Know how the cardiovascular and muscular systems produce energy and how they respond to training—*Level 3*

d.   Understand muscular strength, power, endurance and flexibility; know how each is required of athletes; implement training programs that develop these elements based on the developmental maturity of the athletes—*Level 3*

e. Know common methods of conditioning (such as interval, circuit and weight training) and use each appropriately in preparing a complete conditioning program for athletes—*Level 4*

f. Prepare a comprehensive plan for both in-season and out-of-season conditioning of athletes—*Level 4*

g. Considering the sport being coached and individual differences of athletes, apply the principles of conditioning to the needs of athletes—*Level 5*

Standard 19. Design programs of training and conditioning that properly incorporate the mechanics of movement and sound physiological principles taking into account each individual's ability and medical history, avoiding contraindicated exercises and activities and guarding against the possibility of over-training; be able to modify programs as needed.

a. Know which training/conditioning activities are potentially harmful (contraindicated) for athletes; avoid using these activities in coaching—*Level 2*

b. Know and be able to teach activities that develop and maintain the basic level of conditioning needed for the sport—*Level 2*

c. Know the components of physical fitness and the appropriate levels of each in relation to age and sport-specific demands—*Level 3*

d. Assess the existing sport-specific fitness levels of the athletes—*Level 5*

e. Know how the age, development and needs of athletes determine the appropriate levels of training and conditioning—*Level 4*

f. Identify and use activities that simultaneously provide for more than one area of conditioning—*Level 4*

g. Prepare practice plans that train and condition the entire group while creating opportunities for individual athletes to meet specific needs—*Level 4*

h. Distinguish between minimal and advanced levels of training and conditioning; be able to implement each according to athlete needs—*Level 4*

i. Assess the level of development and interest shown by the athletes for involvement in appropriate off-season conditioning programs—*Level 4*

j. Implement training programs that can be placed in a developmental sequence appropriate for the highly-motivated athlete—*Level 4*

k. Know the indicators of overtraining (i.e. lack of interest in practice, lowered levels of performance, minor injuries failing to heal or chronic complaining about practice or injury); regularly assess the athletes coached for these indicators—*Level 5*

l. Know techniques to mediate/reduce of over-training (i.e. increased variety of drills/activities allowing athletes to organize practices, shortening practice sessions and practicing at different times or in different settings) to reduce or eliminate these symptoms—*Level 5*

m. Know how to prevent over-training; these may include such things as cross-training, periodization and increased autonomy—*Level 5*

Standard 20. Demonstrate knowledge of proper nutrition and educate athletes about the effects of nutrition upon health and physical performance.

a. Know the essential food groups and how to provide a balanced diet for athletes—*Level 3*

b. Know what foods to suggest for a pre-competition meal and when this meal should be eaten—*Level 3*

c. Know the effects on performance of using pharmacological aids such as steroids, amphetamines and caffeine—*Level 4*

d. Understand the demands of athletics as they relate to increased or specialized dietary needs—*Level 4*

e. Know whether dietary supplements are necessary or desirable for athletes—*Level 3*

f. Understand the issues of body composition and weight control and recognize signs of eating disorders—*Level 4*

g. Refer athletes with nutritional problems (such as weight control or use of performance enhancing substances) for appropriate professional assistance—*Level 4*

Standard 21. Demonstrate knowledge of the use and abuse of drugs and promote sound chemical health.

a. Demonstrate/model appropriate behavior regarding sound chemical health. Show concern for the use and abuse of chemicals by athletes and be prepared to intervene—*Level 3*

b. Recognize typical drug use patterns exhibited by athletes and intervene if necessary—*Level 4*

c. Know the legal responsibilities of adults working with minors as they relate to potential use of alcohol, tobacco and other drugs—*Level 3*

d. Know how the use and abuse of chemicals affects athletic performance—*Level 4*

e. Understand the social, emotional and psychological pressures placed upon athletes which make them susceptible to drug use—*Level 4*

f. Plan/facilitate participation by drug free athletes—*Level 4*

g. Know and use appropriate agencies to provide assistance in prevention and treatment of drug use—*Level 3*

h. Know how the side-effects of medically prescribed drugs and medications may affect athletic performance—*Level 4*

Domain: Social/psychological Aspects of Coaching

Standard 22. Subscribe to a philosophy that acknowledges the role of athletics in developing the complete person.

a. Recognize that each athlete is an individual with unique needs and treat athletes accordingly—*Level 3*

b. Organize activities so that athletes have an opportunity to develop/maintain positive feelings of self-worth—*Level 3*

c. Emphasize enjoyment and satisfaction within the context of practices and games, particularly in age group sports—*Level 2*

d. Provide positive encouragement to all athletes on a regular basis—*Level 2*

e. Support participants in developing themselves fully as both athletes and individuals—*Level 3*

f. Allow athletes time and opportunity to participate in a variety of activities outside of sport in support of a balanced lifestyle—*Level 3*

g. Encourage athletes to be well-educated and to become well-rounded individuals—*Level 3*

h. Recognize the connections between sport and other activities in which athletes participate—*Level 3*

i. Assist athletes in learning to manage time appropriately—*Level 4*

j. Identify the ideas and principles guiding your coaching efforts to reflect a concern for the emotional and physical health of your athletes—*Level 4*

Standard 23. Identify and interpret to co-coaches, athletes, concerned others and the general public the values that are to be developed from participation in sports programs.

a. Know the benefits and objectives associated with competitive athletics—*Level 3*

b. Communicate the benefits and objectives of athletics to others at every opportunity—*Level 3*

c. Understand the basic components of good sportsmanship—*Level 2*

d. Require athletes to display good sportsmanship at all times—*Level 2*

e. Relate sportsmanship to complying with the intent of rules, not just the letter of them—*Level 3*

f. Regularly discuss with athletes both actual and hypothetical situations involving ethics in a sport setting—*Level 4*

g. Relate to athletes instances in which ethical conduct translates from sport to life in general—*Level 5*

h. Prepare athletes to deal with media representatives; teach athletes how to interact with persons representing the media in discussions of such issues as evaluation of competition and career objectives—*Level 5*

Standard 24. Identify and apply ethical conduct in sport by maintaining emotional control and demonstrating respect for athletes, officials and other coaches.

a. Exhibit self-control and self-discipline at all times—*Level 3*

b. Recognize the effect coach behavior may have on athletes, officials and spectators; provide a good role model for others—*Level 3*

c. Be positive, courteous and considerate when dealing with others (athletes, officials, opponents, concerned others and spectators) in stressful situations—*Level 3*

d. Know the rules of the sport coached; understand that knowledge of the rules on the part of coaches, athletes and spectators can minimize conflicts with officials and maximize performance—*Level 3*

e. Know that competition requires respect and positive regard by opponents, coaching staffs, officials and spectators—that the conduct of all participants affects the quality of the sport experience for everyone—*Level 3*

f. Learn stress management techniques such as progressive relaxation, deep breathing, behavior modeling, visualization and positive self-talk and be able to teach them to the athletes; assist athletes in using these techniques to deal with competitive stress— *Level 5*

g. Use stress management skills to defuse potentially difficult emotional situations—*Level 5*

Standard 25. Demonstrate effective motivational skills and provide positive, appropriate feedback.

a. Recognize the importance of self-confidence and self-esteem to the athlete's development—*Level 2*

b. Enhance athletes' self-esteem by such methods as showing acceptance, reacting positively to mistakes and giving encouragement— *Level 2*

c. Use a variety of positive instructional methods, such specific feedback and specific encouragement and constructive criticism—*Level 2*

d. Know the social and emotional reasons for people becoming involved in athletics (among these are enjoyment, improving skills and learning new ones, the excitement of competition, being with friends and making new friends and enjoying success and recognition)—*Level 2*

e. Know and use appropriate goal-setting strategies, alternative goals, individual support, arousal techniques, etc.; the positive approach to correcting errors and the questionable function of inspirational speeches as ways of reducing the athletes' fear of failure and so reducing the level of stress felt in practice and competition—*Level 4*

Standard 26. Conduct practices and competitions to enhance the physical, social and emotional growth of athletes.

a. Provide an appropriate model for interacting with teammates, opponents, officials and others—*Level 3*

b. Emphasize the importance of enjoying practices and competitions— *Level 2*

c. Provide opportunities for athletes to derive satisfaction from striving for personal and group goals—*Level 3*

d. Use the sport experience to support positive social behaviors—such as "fair play," sportsmanship, hard work towards group goals, working as a unit, accepting responsibility for success and failure and self-—*Level 3*

e. Develop positive social behaviors in athletes by acknowledging acts of sportsmanship, encouraging respect for teammates and opponents, respecting effort and improvement and stressing personal involvement and self-control—*Level 3*

f. Structure practice and game experiences so that participants find them satisfying, positive experiences that provide an opportunity to develop the positive values associated with competition—*Level 3*

Standard 27. Be sufficiently familiar with the basic principles of goal setting to motivate athletes toward immediate and long range goals.

a. Recognize the difference between short and long-range goals— *Level 3*

b. Help athletes prepare short and long-range goals for themselves and their team, recognizing that goal setting can have both positive and negative consequences—*Level 4*

c. Prepare short and long-range coaching goals—*Level 3*

d. Assist athletes in relating long-range goals for participation to the realities of competition and the need to develop non-sports related interests and talents—*Level 5*

Standard 28. Treat each athlete as an individual while recognizing the dynamic relationship of personality and socio-cultural variables such as gender, race and socio-economic differences.

a. Recognize that social environment influences the behaviors and personalities of athletes—*Level 5*

b. Understand how social, cultural and emotional forces interact in creating athlete personalities—*Level 5*

c. Understand the many dimensions of personality that may be expressed in athletics and teach athletes how to deal with these differences—*Level 5*

d. Accept differences in personality as another necessary component in preparing athletes for competition—*Level 5*

e. Promote the equality of opportunity within the sport by encouraging participation regardless of race, gender, socio-economic status or culture; this may involve working to overcome such barriers as tradition, bias, public image, funding, regulations, policies and apathy—*Level 4*

Standard 29. Identify desirable behaviors and structure experiences to develop such behaviors in each athlete.

a. Model desirable behaviors and use a variety of skills appropriate to specific situations—*Level 3*

b. Allow all athletes to fill leadership positions at appropriate times— *Level 3*

c. Identify desirable behaviors exhibited by athletes; these may include the ability to plan and organize activities, charisma, enthusiasm and the ability to help teammates perform better—*Level 4*

d. Distinguish between positive (planning and organizing skills, enthusiasm) and negative (bullying, dictatorial) behaviors; utilize and encourage the former and avoid and discourage the latter— *Level 3*

e. Prepare practice and season plans that establish and reinforce the development of desirable behavior for all athletes—*Level 4*

Domain: Skills, Tactics and Strategies

Standard 30. Identify and apply specific competitive tactics and strategies appropriate for the age and skill levels involved.

a. Know and identify both efficient and inefficient performances of the basic skills of the sport; be able to analyze and correct typical errors in performance—*Level 3*

b. Know all the rules of the sport and teach them to athletes—*Level 3*

c. Know the vocabulary necessary to communicate with coaches and athletes—*Level 3*

d. Know the basic strategies and tactics of the sport; be able to apply them in appropriate situations—*Level 3*

e. Understand that the athlete's ability to use tactics and understand strategies are developmental and that athletes must master basic ones before learning advanced strategies and tactics—*Level 4*

f. Select strategies and tactics based upon the age, skill, experience and conditioning level of the athletes—*Level 3*

g. Recognize that the performance of skills and techniques is determined by the athlete's maturity and experience—*Level 3*

h. Prepare situationally-specific plans that reflect the abilities of the athletes—*Level 4*

i. Prepare end-of-contest and special situation strategies for use as needed—*Level 4*

j. Understand how rules may dictate strategy, and be able to implement appropriate strategies in competitive situations—*Level 5*

Standard 31. Organize and implement materials for scouting, planning practices and analysis of games.

a. Implement both seasonal and daily practice plans—*Level 3*

b. Summarize, evaluate and maintain records of drills and practice plans used—*Level 3*

c. Recognize the necessity of scouting opponents at upper levels of play in many sports—*Level 4*

d. Be able to scout opponents, assess and analyze strengths and weaknesses, and document information in a usable form—*Level 4*

e. Demonstrate the ability to develop a competition plan based on assessment of opponents and the athlete's abilities—*Level 4*

f. Prepare a written game plan summary that considers opponent tendencies and identifies strategies and tactics for positive results—*Level 4*

g. Develop and use meaningful aids for analysis of competitions; these should include such information as individual and team statistics, videotapes and assessments by observers—*Level 4*

h. Be able to anticipate the likely strategies of opposing coaches and be prepared to respond to them in a timely manner—*Level 5*

i. Be able to identify the basic philosophy guiding the play of opponents—*Level 5*

j. Use knowledge of the opponent strategies, tactics and philosophy to aid in the preparation of game plans and the selection of strategies and tactics—*Level 5*

Standard 32. Understand and enforce the rules and regulations of appropriate bodies that govern sport and education.

a. Know the rules and regulations (of relevant governing bodies) concerning participation in the sport—*Level 3*

b. Strictly enforce the rules of the governing body—especially as they relate to athlete eligibility to participate—*Level 3*

c. Properly complete all forms validating the eligibility of athletes—*Level 2*

d. Develop and maintain a system for keeping athlete records current and secure—*Level 3*

Standard 33. Organize, conduct and evaluate practice sessions with regard to established program goals that are appropriate for different stages of the season.

a. Determine which skills in each area of the sport experience—physical skills, knowledge of the sport, physical fitness and personal/social skills—are to be taught at each level within the total program—*3*

b. Arrange these skills and introduce them in a logical sequence; use a season planning calendar to indicate when each skill or tactic will be taught—*Level 3*

c. Teach the skills and tactics through practice activities that reflect competitive experiences—*Level 5*

d. Stress performance as the measure of progress in learning skills—*Level 5*

e. After the competitive season, summarize and analyze successes and areas needing improvement—*Level 3*

f. Use season analysis and summary along with the seasonal and individual practice schedules to assist in planning for the succeeding season—*Level 5*

g. Evaluate the progress of individual athletes in achieving pre-determined goals—*Level 5*

h. Consult with experienced coaches and educators for aid in assessing the athlete progress—*Level 5*

Domain: Teaching and Administration

Standard 34. Know the key elements of sport principles and technical skills as well as the various teaching methods that can be used to introduce and refine them.

a. Know the key elements of effective practice plans and prepare sample seasonal, weekly and daily plans; include a variety of activities and drills in daily plans—*Level 3*

b. Know the techniques of corrective action and personnel management that are appropriate to the age of the athletes being coached—*Level 3*

c. Know and apply steps for systematically instructing athletes as they progress developmentally in the skills of the sport—*Level 4, Level 5*

d. Demonstrate the ability to communicate effectively, using appropriate available technology—*Level 3*

e. Learn and apply the elements of effective instruction—*Level 3*

f. Prepare a set of desired outcomes for the sport coached; these should emphasize athlete growth and development—*Level 4*

g. Sequence practices so that all athletes develop a sense of self-control and discipline as they become increasingly responsible for themselves and elements of practice—*Level 3*

h. Evaluate drills based on their effectiveness in developing skills and tactics appropriate for the level of competition—*Level 3*

i. Determine when it is necessary to re-instruct athletes in such elements as skills, strategies and rules—*Level 5*

j. Know and use the most effective instructional techniques of re-teaching—*Level 5*

k. Know and use different motivational techniques and reward systems in preparing athletes for sessions involving re-instruction and review—*Level 5*

l. Use appropriate tools such as videotapes to analyze skills and to monitor skills in both practice and competition settings—*Level 5*

m. Use assessment during practice to guide instruction and re-instruction—*Level 5*

Standard 35. Demonstrate objective and effective procedures for the evaluation and selection of personnel involved in the athletic program and for periodic program reviews.

a. Identify the desirable characteristics and abilities to be attained by each athlete throughout the season—*Level 3*

b. Consider the desired characteristics and abilities when preparing regular evaluations of the athletes—as they try out, during the season and at the end of the season—*Level 3*

c. Provide athletes with evaluations of personal achievement and discuss the results with each athlete individually at regular intervals—*Level 3*

d. Evaluate the effectiveness of coaching techniques used as they relate to the performance of athletes—*Level 3*

e. Understand that coaching effectiveness is determined by the degree to which athletes meet previously established objectives and that both peer and self-evaluation are effective tools—*Level 3*

f. Follow an established sequence for evaluation which involves the identification of objectives, data collection, analysis of data and making the needed changes—*Level 4*

g. Record data about athlete performance (such as a checklist of effective coaching actions and records of progress by the athletes) in order to monitor progress and coaching effectiveness—*Level 4*

h. Establish criteria for the selection and elimination of members of a team or squad; apply these criteria with fairness and integrity— *Level 4*

i. Prepare job descriptions for assistants, managers, team captains, etc.—*Level 4*

j. Prepare a list of performance objectives for additional personnel— *Level 5*

k. Evaluate program personnel—including assistant coaches, managers and trainers—*Level 4*

l. Use formal, written evaluations to assist in selecting and retaining program personnel—*Level 5*

m. Know and be able to implement diplomatic, sensitive ways in which to communicate with program personnel—athletes trying out, players, co-coaches and others—about their status and or performance— *Level 4*

Domain: Professional Preparation and Development

Standard 36. Demonstrate organizational and administrative efficiency in implementing sports programs, e.g. event management, budgetary procedures, facility maintenance, participation in public relations activities.

a. Organize and conduct effective meetings before, during and after the season; these meetings—for such groups as athletes, staff, guardians and alumni—can be used to prevent, solve or manage problems of the group—*Level 3*

b. Maintain informal, personal contacts designed to collect information and keep open lines of communication among all parties— *Level 2*

c. Use appropriate administrative forms related to (but not necessarily limited to) physical examinations for athletes, emergency procedures, injury reports, parents' meetings, program evaluation, facility scheduling, travel and budgeting—*Level 2*

d. Regularly inspect equipment and know how to arrange for repair/replacement as needed—*Level 2*

e. Establish record keeping procedures to account for sports equipment and its maintenance—*Level 4*

f. Be involved in public relations activities within both the sport and the community—*Level 4*

g. Recognize the need for preparing and maintaining administrative records; maintain such records; store them for the required period of time—*Level 3*

h. Demonstrate the ability to manage the key elements of contests; these include inspecting and approving facilities, transportation, competitors, crowd control, locker room supervision and public relations—*Level 4*

i. Develop and maintain a record keeping system for administrative forms and correspondence—*Level 4*

Standard 37. Acquire sufficient practical field experience and supervision in the essential coaching areas to ensure an adequate level of coaching competence for the level of sport coached. This would include a variety of knowledge, skills and experiences. The coach should:

a. Know the appropriate sequence used to teach necessary skills to developing athletes and the means for assessing the skill level and progress of athletes—*Level 5*

b. Prepare a season plan considering the abilities of in-coming athletes and maximum facilitation of their skills during the season—*Level 5*

c. Prepare practice plans that reflect reasonable time allowances for skill development in consideration of the sequential nature of skill acquisition—*Level 5*

d. Prepare written practice plans that follow guidelines for effective instruction and meeting the athlete needs—*Level 5*

e. Evaluate athletes during practice sessions; identify those who are able to enter higher levels of competition on the basis of predetermined criteria, such as skill, ability, adherence to rules and social/psychological considerations—*Level 5*

f. Assign positions, events and develop line-ups, orders and rotations that reflect the capabilities and readiness of the athletes—*Level 5*

g. Select skills and strategies appropriate to the sport and choose those that are consistent with athlete abilities—*Level 5*

h. Make appropriate coaching decisions during competition and adjust decisions based on situation—such as changes in strategy or tactics, safety considerations or competitive flow—*Level 5*

i. Teach the rules governing competition to all athletes—*Level 5*

j. Evaluate team play and individual performance in order to correct errors and facilitate maximum performance—*Level 5*

k. Evaluate player development and team play over the course of a season—*Level 5*

l. Deal effectively and sensitively with parents and guardians and/or others concerned with individual athletes—*Level 5*

m. Relate positively to officials, opposing coaches and athletes, and spectators—*Level 5*

n. Be aware of current developments in the sport through attending clinics and workshops, reading professional publications and communicating with other coaches and professionals—*Level 5*

o. Utilize guidelines for effective instruction—*Level 5*

p. Emphasize and foster self-control and self-discipline by athletes—*Level 5*

q. Evaluate effectiveness of drills—*Level 5*

r. Prepare desired outcomes for the athletic program which emphasize the growth and development of athletes—*Level 5*

s. Sequence practices so that athletes become increasingly responsible for themselves and elements of practice—*Level 5*

t.   Demonstrate the ability to communicate effectively using audio-visual resources—*Level 5*

u.   Take advantage of educational opportunities related to non-sport specific aspects of coaching—*Level 2*

v.   At regular intervals, seek feedback from experienced coaches or assistants to evaluate practice sessions; discuss their observations and implement changes—*Level 5*

w.   Scout opponents and use the information for planning contests as appropriate—*Level 4*

x.   Apply scientific and experiential information to the improvement of the specific sport—*Level 5*

y.   Participate in appropriate professional sport or coaching organizations at the local, state, regional and national levels—*Level 4*

z.   Know the techniques for re-teaching and the motivational problems associated with re-teaching—*Level 4*

aa.   Incorporate assessment and re-teaching into practices and competitions—*Level 5*

National Standards for Athletic Coaches

Five Levels of Coaching Competency

Introduction to Levels

As previously mentioned, the eight domains, 37 standards and approximately 320 competencies of the **National Standards for Athletic Coaches** are represented in five levels of coaching practice. Level 1 represents what every coach should know and be able to do before ever starting their first coaching responsibility.

Each level after Level 1 increases the knowledge and abilities of which a coach should be aware, be able to apply or master at that particular level. Thus, it is the responsibility of a coach, after mastery of a competency, to continue to refine and internalize those competencies for all subsequent levels.

Thus, after a competency has been mastered, it will not appear in the next level(s). The competencies mastered at each level should continue to be reviewed, refined and internalized as development of coaching expertise is not static, but requires continual professional development at the next level(s). A coach at Level 5 must know/master all competencies of the **National Standards** and continue efforts to stay up to date with new information about all aspects of coaching.

Model Competencies
Level 1

Domain: Injuries: Prevention, Care and Management

Standard 1. Prevent injuries by recognizing and insisting on safe playing conditions.

a. Recognize the environmental and safety hazards likely to affect athletes in practice and competition—such as wet or slippery surfaces, structures in or near activity areas with which athletes may collide, such as walls, fences and goals standards, sprinkler heads or spectator seating—*Mastery*

b. Establish and follow procedures for identifying and correcting unsafe conditions—*Mastery*

c. Stop or modify practice or play when unsafe conditions exist—*Mastery*

d. Ensure that qualified individuals are present to officiate all competitions—*Mastery*

e. Require the use of appropriate and adequate safety equipment by all athletes during practice and competition—*Mastery*

f. Know and apply the rules and policies related to the safety and welfare of athletes in the sport being coached during all practices and competition—*Mastery*

Standard 2. Ensure that protective equipment is in good condition, fits properly and is worn as prescribed by the manufacturer; ensure that equipment and facilities meet required standards (ASTM and USCPSC).

a. Know what safety equipment and facilities are needed by athletes and required by rules governing competition in the sport coached or otherwise needed for athletic protection—*Mastery*

b. Assist athletes in choosing, fitting and maintaining equipment—including safety gear—*Mastery*

Standard 3. Recognize that proper conditioning and good health are vital to the prevention of athletic injuries.

b. Use conditioning drills and activities consistent with the needs of the sport and athlete—*Mastery*

Standard 4. Prevent exposure to the risk of injuries by considering the effects of environmental conditions on the circulatory and respiratory systems when planning and scheduling practices and contests and implementing programs for physical conditioning.

f. Provide for unlimited fluid/water intake during physical activity andinstruct athletes about proper hydration and acclemitization—*Awareness*

g. Know the most common pre-existing conditions of athletes, e.g. asthma, allergies, diabetes, improper body fat levels, nutritional deficiencies, cardiac conditions, seizures, repeated concussion, serious orthopedic injury; how to identify those athletes suffering from these conditions; the circumstances in which these conditions put the athlete at unusual risk; how to moderate activity to effectively reduce that risk; how to recognize smptoms indicating that the condition is causing the athlete to suffer activity related injury/illness; and how to appropriately respond to such indications—Awareness

Standard 5. Be able to plan, coordinate and implement procedures for appropriate emergency care.

a. Know the details of and be prepared to execute the established emergency plan for the organization/activity/situation—*Mastery*

b. Have available a written emergency plan for all sites where practices and competitions occur—*Awareness*

c. Maintain appropriate medical records for each athlete—including medical information or physical examination forms and medical treatment consent forms—*Mastery*

d. Assure that medical information and treatment consent forms are available during all practices and competition—*Mastery*

Standard 6. Demonstrate skill in the prevention, recognition and evaluation of injuries and the ability to assist athletes with the recovery/rehabilitation from injuries that are generally associated with participation in athletics in accordance with guidelines provided by qualified medical personnel.

Prevention

a. Recognize the physical risks in the sport to be coached and how injuries may be prevented or minimized and the importance of reporting all symptoms immediately—*Mastery*

Care

d. Have knowledge of first aid and CPR, or have immediate access to someone who is first aid/CPR qualified—*Mastery*

e. Know how to recognize and respond to symptoms of injuries that may occur in the sport coached— *Mastery*

f. Have a first aid kit available at all practices and games; know its contents and their appropriate use; know the location of the nearest telephone— *Mastery*

g. Know and be able to apply standard management procedures designed to minimize exposure to blood-borne pathogens (BBPs); know and follow specific contest rules intended to limit exposure of athletes and officials to blood or bodily fluids— *Mastery*

h. Know when professional medical care is required for an injured athlete— *Mastery*

i. Complete and file an injury report form for each medical emergency— *Mastery*

Management

j. Follow guidelines and instructions provided by a NATA certified athletic trainer, team physician and/or other qualified sports medicine professionals in implementation of procedures for returning athletes to play following injury or illness, including when the athlete can resume activity—*Awareness*

q. Allow athletes the time to recover fully from injury before returning to play— *Mastery*

Standard 7: Facilitate a unified medical program of prevention, care and management of injuries by coordinating the roles and actions of the coach and a NATA certified athletic trainer with those of a physician.

Care

g. Assure that an athlete is referred to the NATA Certified athletic trainer, team physician or other qualified provider upon sustaining an injury which requires more than minor first aid care, and does not return to activity without clearance from such provider(s)— *Mastery*

Domain: Risk Management

Standard 9. Understand the scope of legal responsibilities that comes with assuming a coaching position, e. g. proper supervision, planning and instruction, matching participants, safety, first aid and risk management.

a. Follow safety guidelines, procedures and risk management plans established by program administrators—*Mastery*

b. In accordance with established administrative procedures and based upon relevant legal requirements, organize and maintain appropriate records as evidence in the event of legal challenges. Records should include assignments of personnel; practice plans; special safety measures; attendance of athletes; emergency plans;, safety rules/procedures; reports of injuries; copies of records of all oral and written communications concerning an injury or other unusual event)—*Mastery*

c. Provide proper general and specific supervision of athletes— *Mastery*

d. Inspect facilities and equipment for potential safety hazards prior to each use—*Mastery*

e. Know the coaches responsibilities in first aid, CPR and emergency procedures—*Mastery*

f. Know the legal responsibilities of the coach in teaching, supervision, transportation, medical care and communication and how to meet them—*Mastery*

g. Be able to match participants in terms of such characteristics as age, maturity, size, skill and experience; group participants appropriately—*Awareness*

Standard 10. Properly inform coaching assistants, parent/guardians and athletes of the inherent risks associated with sport so that decisions about participation can be made with informed consent.

a. Know the specific risks to participants and how to reduce these risks for the sport coached—*Mastery*

b. Inform those involved about the risks of athletics by instructing athletes and others concerned in the purpose of agreements to participate and informed consent, medical information, medical release and medical emergency forms—*Mastery*

c. Prior to participation, require the completion of all necessary agreements and medical forms by athletes and guardians—*Awareness*

d. For coaches and participants, conduct and document meetings regarding procedures for safety and emergency and guidelines for risk management—*Awareness*

Standard 11. Know and convey the need and availability of appropriate medical insurance.

b. Discuss the importance of adequate health and accident insurance coverage with athletes and parents/guardians prior to participation and as needed at other times—*Mastery*

c. Comply with existing requirements regarding insurance for athletic participation and record evidence that all participants have such coverage—*Mastery*

Standard 12. Participate in continuing education regarding rules changes, improvements in equipment, philosophical changes, better techniques and other information in order to enhance the health, safety and success of the athlete.

a. Attend rules meetings offered by appropriate sanctioning groups in order to be informed of rules changes and interpretations—*Mastery*

e. Document formal and informal education as evidence of accumulated competence—*Mastery*

Domain: Growth, Development and Learning

Standard 13. Recognize the developmental physical changes that occur as athletes move from youth through adulthood and know how these changes influence the sequential learning and performance of motor skills in a specific sport.

b. Recognize the physical and motor limitations of athletes common to the age and skill level being coached and adjust expectations accordingly—*Awareness*

c. Choose drills and practice plans which allow athletes the opportunity to improve while not forcing them to extend themselves beyond their physical and mental-emotional limits—*Awareness*

d. Teach skills and strategies that are within the performance limits of the athletes—*Awareness*

Standard 14. Understand the social and emotional development of the athletes being coached, know how to recognize problems related to this development and know where to refer them for appropriate assistance when necessary.

b. Know the different general stages of social and emotional development of the athletes being coached and realize the developmental differences that may exist—*Awareness*

c. Be aware of social-psychological issues that may affect athletes of different ages in contemporary society; these may include such factors as peer pressure, lowered self-esteem, single-parent families, substance abuse, violence, sexual identity, emotional stress and child abuse—*Awareness*

Standard 15. Analyze human performance in terms of developmental information and individual body structure.

b. Assess athlete success in learning skills relative to their physical limits—*Mastery*

c. Develop practice plans that allow for all athletes to learn new skills at their own pace and within their own limits—*Awareness*

Standard 16. Provide instruction to develop sport-specific motor skills. Refer athletes to appropriate counsel as needed.

b Emphasize life-long activity and enjoyment of physical activity as goals of athletic participation—*Awareness*

d. Refer athletes with developmental motor problems for appropriate professional assistance—*Awareness*

Standard 17. Provide learning experiences appropriate to the growth and development of the age group coached.

a. Acquire or prepare season objectives that reflect the physical and mental development and levelsof the athletes—*Awareness*

b. Select specific drills and activities that allow athletes of various levels to experience success—*Awareness*

Domain: Training, Conditioning and Nutrition

Standard 19. Design programs of training and conditioning that properly incorporate the mechanics of movement and sound physiological principles taking into account each individual's ability and medical

history, avoiding contraindicated exercises and activities and guarding against the possibility of over-training; be able to modify programs as needed.

a. Know which training/conditioning activities are potentially harmful (contraindicated) for athletes; avoid using these activities in coaching—*Application*

b. Know and be able to teach activities that develop and maintain the basic level of conditioning needed for the sport—*Application*

c. Know the components of physical fitness and the appropriate levels of each in relation to age and sport-specific demands—*Awareness*

Standard 21. Demonstrate knowledge of the use and abuse of drugs and promote sound chemical health.

c. Know the legal responsibilities of adults working with minors as they relate to potential use of alcohol, tobacco and other drugs—*Awareness*

Domain: Social/psychological Aspects of Coaching

Standard 22. Subscribe to a philosophy that acknowledges the role of athletics in developing the complete person.

a. Recognize that each athlete is an individual with unique needs and treat athletes accordingly—*Awareness*

b. Organize activities so that athletes have an opportunity to develop/maintain positive feelings of self-worth—*Awareness*

c. Emphasize enjoyment and satisfaction within the context of practices and games, particularly in age group sports—*Application*

d. Provide positive encouragement to all athletes on a regular basis—*Awareness*

e. Support participants in developing themselves fully as both athletes and individuals—*Awareness*

Standard 23. Identify and interpret to co-coaches, athletes, concerned others and the general public the values that are to be developed from participation in sports programs.

a. Know the benefits and objectives associated with competitive athletics—*Awareness*

b. Communicate the benefits and objectives of athletics to others at every opportunity—*Awareness*

c. Understand the basic components of good sportsmanship—*Awareness*

d. Require athletes to display good sportsmanship at all times—*Awareness*

Standard 24. Identify and apply ethical conduct in sport by maintaining emotional control and demonstrating respect for athletes, officials and other coaches.

a. Exhibit self-control and self-discipline at all times—*Awareness*

b. Recognize the effect a coach's behavior may have on athletes, officials and spectators; provide a good role model for others—*Awareness*

c. Be positive, courteous and considerate when dealing with others (athletes, officials, opponents, concerned others and spectators) in stressful situations—*Awareness*

d. Know the rules of the sport coached; understand that knowledge of the rules on the part of coaches, athletes and spectators can minimize conflicts with officials and maximize performance—*Awareness*

e. Know that competition requires respect and positive regard by opponents, coaching staffs, officials and spectators—that the conduct of all participants affects the quality of the sport experience for everyone—*Awareness*

Standard 25. Demonstrate effective motivational skills and provide positive, appropriate feedback.

a. Recognize the importance of self-confidence and self-esteem to the athlete development—*Awareness*

b. Enhance athletes' self-esteem by such methods as showing acceptance, reacting positively to mistakes and giving encouragement—*Application*

c. Use a variety of positive instructional methods, such specific feedback and specific encouragement and constructive criticism—*Application*

d. Know the social and emotional reasons for people becoming involved in athletics (among these are enjoyment, improving skills and learning new ones, the excitement of competition, being with friends and making new friends and enjoying success and recognition)—*Awareness*

Standard 26. Conduct practices and competitions to enhance the physical, social and emotional growth of athletes.

a. Provide an appropriate model for interacting with teammates, opponents, officials and others—*Awareness*

b. Emphasize the importance of enjoying practices and competitions—*Awareness*

c. Provide opportunities for athletes to derive satisfaction from striving for personal and group goals—*Awareness*

f. Structure practice and game experiences so that participants find them satisfying, positive experiences that provide an opportunity to develop the positive values associated with competition—*Awareness*

Standard 29. Identify desirable behaviors and structure experiences to develop such behaviors in each athlete.

a. Model desirable behaviors and use a variety of skills appropriate to specific situations—*Awareness*

b. Allow all athletes to fill leadership positions at appropriate times—*Awareness*

Domain: Skills, Tactics and Strategies

Standard 30. Identify and apply specific competitive tactics and strategies appropriate for the age and skill levels involved.

a. Know and identify both efficient and inefficient performances of the basic skills of the sport; be able to analyze and correct typical errors in performance—*Awareness*

b. Know all the rules of the sport and teach them to athletes—*Awareness*

c. Know the vocabulary necessary to communicate with coaches and athletes—*Awareness*

d. Know the basic strategies and tactics of the sport; be able to apply them in appropriate situations—*Awareness*

f. Select strategies and tactics based upon the age, skill, experience and conditioning level of the athletes—*Awareness*

Standard 31. Organize and implement materials for scouting, planning practices and analysis of games.

a. Implement both seasonal and daily practice plans—*Awareness*

Standard 32. Understand and enforce the rules and regulations of appropriate bodies that govern sport and education.

a. Know the rules and regulations (of relevant governing bodies) concerning participation in the sport—*Awareness*

b. Strictly enforce the rules of the governing body—especially as they relate to athlete eligibility to participate—*Awareness*

c. Properly complete all forms validating the eligibility of athletes—*Application*

Standard 33. Organize, conduct and evaluate practice sessions with regard to established program goals that are appropriate for different stages of the season.

a. Determine which skills in each area of the sport experience—physical skills, knowledge of the sport, physical fitness and personal/social skills—are to be taught at each level within the total program—*Awareness*

b. Arrange these skills and introduce them in a logical sequence; use a season planning calendar to indicate when each skill or tactic will be taught—*Awareness*

• •

e.   After the competitive season, summarize and analyze successes
      and areas needing improvement—*Awareness*

Domain: Teaching and Administration

**Standard 34. Know the key elements of sport princi-
ples and technical skills as well as the various teaching methods that can be used to introduce and refine
them.**

a.   Know the key elements of effective practice plans and prepare sam-
      ple seasonal, weekly and daily plans; include a variety of activities
      and drills in daily plans—*Awareness*
b.   Know the techniques of corrective action and personnel manage-
      ment that are appropriate to the age of the athletes being
      coached—*Awareness*
c.   Know and apply steps for systematically instructing athletes as
      they progress developmentally in the skills of the sport—*Awareness*
d.   Demonstrate the ability to communicate effectively, using appro-
      priate available technology—*Awareness*

Domain: Professional Preparation and Development

**Standard 36. Demonstrate organizational and
administrative efficiency in implementing sports
programs, e. g. event management, budgetary procedures, facility maintenance, participation in public
relations activities.**

a.   Organize and conduct effective meetings before, during and after
      the season; these meetings—for such groups as athletes, staff,
      guardians and alumni—can be used to prevent, solve or manage
      problems of the group—*Application*
b.   Maintain informal, personal contacts designed to collect informa-
      tion and keep open lines of communication among all parties—
      Application
c.   Use appropriate administrative forms related to (but not necessar-
      ily limited to) physical examinations for athletes, emergency proce-
      dures, injury reports, parents' meetings, program evaluation,
      facility scheduling, travel and budgeting—*Application*
d.   Regularly inspect equipment and know how to arrange for
      repair/replacement as needed—*Application*

Model for Competencies
Level 2

Domain: Injuries: Prevention, Care and Management

Standard 1. Prevent injuries by recognizing and insisting on safe playing conditions.

g.   Know that safety equipment, coach's vigilance and other safeguards provide protection against injury to athletes—*Awareness*

Standard 2. Ensure that protective equipment is in good condition, fits properly and is worn as prescribed by the manufacturer; ensure that equipment and facilities meet required standards (ASTM and USCPSC).

c.   Know which items of equipment are subject to recognized safety standards (ASTM, USCPSC) and ensure that all items meet these standards—*Mastery*

d.   Know applicable safety standards for the sport coached; regularly inspect all apparel and equipment for conformance—*Mastery*

Standard 3. Recognize that proper conditioning and good health are vital to the prevention of athletic injuries.

f.   Prepare a season coaching plan that indicates when and how conditioning will take place—*Awareness*

Standard 4. Prevent exposure to the risk of injuries by considering the effects of environmental conditions on the circulatory and respiratory systems when planning and scheduling practices and contests and implementing programs for physical conditioning.

b.   Recognize the differences of athlete response to circulatory/respiratory stress—*Awareness*

c.   Know how such environmental factors as temperature, humidity, altitude and general climate can represent a risk to athletes and how such risk can be reduced—*Awareness*

d.   Know how clothing worn for practice and competition can affect the risks associated with various environmental conditions—*Awareness*

e.   Prepare practice plans that allow for dealing with dangerous environmental factors; be prepared to limit activity to reduce risk—*Awareness*

f.   Provide for unlimited fluid/water intake during physical activity andinstruct athletes about proper hydration and acclemitization— *Application*

g.   Know the most common pre-existing conditions of athletes, e.g. asthma, allergies, diabetes, improper body fat levels, nutritional deficiencies, cardiac conditions, seizures, repeated concussion, serious orthopedic injury; how to identify those athletes suffering from these conditions; the circumstances in which these conditions put the athlete at unusual risk; how to moderate activity to effectively reduce that risk; how to recognize smptoms indicating that the condition is causing the athlete to suffer activity related injury/illness; and how to appropriately respond to such indications—*Application*

Standard 5. Be able to plan, coordinate and implement procedures for appropriate emergency care.

b.   Have available a written emergency plan for all sites where practices and competitions occur—*Mastery*

Standard 6. Demonstrate skill in the prevention, recognition and evaluation of injuries and the ability to assist athletes with the recovery/rehabilitation from injuries that are generally associated with participation in athletics in accordance with guidelines provided by qualified medical personnel.

Prevention

b.   Prepare practice plans that indicate where and when dangerous situations may arise and tell how these situations are to be managed—*Mastery*

Management

j.   Follow guidelines and instructions provided by a NATA certified athletic trainer, team physician and/or other qualified sports medicine professionals in implementation of procedures for returning athletes to play following injury or illness, including when the athlete can resume activity—*Mastery*

Standard 7. Facilitate a unified medical program of prevention, care and management of injuries by coordinating the roles and actions of the coach and a NATA certified athletic trainer with those of the physician.

Prevention

a.   Consult with a NATA certified athletic trainer or physician for assistance in understanding the physical needs of athletes—*Mastery*

b.   Change coaching techniques when a trainer or physician brings the need to do so to the coach's attention—*Mastery*

Care

f. Assure that an athlete is referred to a NATA Certified athletic trainer, team physician or other qualified provider upon sustaining an injury which requires more than minor first aid care, and that the athlete does not return to activity without clearance from such provider(s). —*Mastery*

Management

g. Keep a record of communications with health-care providers concerned with the treatment of injured athletes—*Mastery*

Standard 8. Provide coaching assistants, athletes and parents/guardians with education about injury prevention, injury reporting and sources of medical care.

b. Know sources of information that can be shared with assistant coaches and parent/guardians concerning the care and treatment of injured athletes—*Application*

c. Encourage assistant coaches and parent/guardians to participate in educational programs that emphasize the prevention, reporting and care of injuries—*Awareness*

Domain: Risk Management

Standard 9. Understand the scope of legal responsibilities that comes with assuming a coaching position, e. g. proper supervision, planning and instruction, matching participants, safety, first aid and risk management.

g. Be able to match participants in terms of such characteristics as age, maturity, size, skill and experience; group participants appropriately—*Application*

h. Cooperate with administrators and medical providers in developing and regularly reviewing a formal risk management plan—*Mastery*

Standard 10. Properly inform coaching assistants, parent/guardians and athletes of the inherent risks associated with sport so that decisions about participation can be made with informed consent.

c. Prior to participation, require the completion of all necessary agreements and medical forms by athletes and guardians—*Mastery*

d. For coaches and participants, conduct and document meetings regarding procedures for safety and emergency and guidelines for risk management—*Mastery*

Standard 11. Know and convey the need and availability of appropriate medical insurance.

a. Distribute information to assistant coaches, athletes and parent/guardians concerned about sources for personal health and liability insurance—*Mastery*

Domain: Growth, Development and Learning

Standard 13. Recognize the developmental physical changes that occur as athletes move from youth through adulthood and know how these changes influence the sequential learning and performance of motor skills in a specific sport.

a. Demonstrate knowledge of the general developmental sequence in mental, motor and physical abilities—*Awareness*
b. Recognize the physical and motor limitations of athletes common to the age and skill level being coached and adjust expectations accordingly—*Application*
c. Choose drills and practice plans which allow athletes the opportunity to improve while not forcing them to extend themselves beyond their physical and mental-emotional limits—*Application*
d. Teach skills and strategies that are within the performance limits of the athletes—*Application*

Standard 14. Understand the social and emotional development of the athletes being coached, know how to recognize problems related to this development and know where to refer them for appropriate assistance when necessary.

a. Recognize the typical behaviors exhibited by athletes of the age groups being coached—*Application*
b. Know the different general stages of social and emotional development of the athletes being coached and realize the developmental differences that may exist—*Application*
c. Be aware of social-psychological issues that may affect athletes of different ages in contemporary society; these may include such factors as peer pressure, lowered self-esteem, single-parent families, substance abuse, violence, sexual identity, emotional stress and child abuse—*Application*
d. Know how to recognize psycho-social distress and the resources available to assist athletes—*Awareness*
f. Know and educate athletes and parent/guardian how social psychological problems may increase susceptibility to injuries or influence recovery—*Awareness*

Standard 15. Analyze human performance in terms of developmental information and individual body structure.

a. Assess the capabilities of athletes based on age, matureity, size, skill level and experience—*Mastery*

c.   Develop practice plans that allow for all athletes to learn new skills at their own pace and within their own limits—*Mastery*

d.   Recognize that athlete performance is determined by developmental level, chronological age, experience and genetic endowment—*Awareness*

Standard 16. Provide instruction to develop sport-specific motor skills. Refer athletes to appropriate counsel as needed.

b.   Emphasize life-long activity and enjoyment of physical activity as goals of athletic participation—*Application*

d.   Refer athletes with developmental motor problems for appropriate professional assistance—*Mastery*

Standard 17. Provide learning experiences appropriate to the growth and development of the age group coached.

a.   Acquire or prepare season objectives that reflect the physical and mental development and levelsof the athletes—*Application*

b.   Select specific drills and activities that allow athletes of various levels to experience success—*Application*

c.   Use a variety of activities to help athletes of various levels of ability develop specific skills—*Awareness*

Domain: Training, Conditioning and Nutrition

Standard 18. Demonstrate a basic knowledge of physiological systems and their responses to training and conditioning.

a.   Know the five essentials of conditioning: Warm up/cool down, overload, progression, specificity and reversibility; implement them according to the developmental level of the athletes—*Awareness*

Standard 19. Design programs of training and conditioning that properly incorporate the mechanics of movement and sound physiological principles taking into account each individual's ability and medical history, avoiding contraindicated exercises and activities and guarding against the possibility of over-training; be able to modify programs as needed.

a.   Know which training/conditioning activities are potentially harmful (contraindicated) for athletes; avoid using these activities in coaching—*Mastery*

b.   Know and be able to teach activities that develop and maintain the basic level of conditioning needed for the sport—*Mastery*

c.   Know the components of physical fitness and the appropriate levels of each in relation to age and sport-specific demands—*Application*

Standard 20. Demonstrate knowledge of proper nutrition and educate athletes about the effects of nutrition upon health and physical performance

a. Know the essential food groups and how to provide a balanced diet for athletes—*Awareness*

b. Know what foods to suggest for a pre-competition meal and when this meal should be eaten—*Application*

Standard 21. Demonstrate knowledge of the use and abuse of drugs and promote sound chemical health.

b. Recognize typical drug use patterns exhibited by athletes and intervene if necessary—*Awareness*

c. Know the legal responsibilities of adults working with minors as they relate to potential use of alcohol, tobacco and other drugs—*Application*

Domain: Social/psychological Aspects of Coaching

Standard 22. Subscribe to a philosophy that acknowledges the role of athletics in developing the complete person.

a. Recognize that each athlete is an individual with unique needs and treat athletes accordingly—*Application*

b. Organize activities so that athletes have an opportunity to develop/maintain positive feelings of self-worth—*Application*

c. Emphasize enjoyment and satisfaction within the context of practices and games, particularly in age group sports—*Mastery*

d. Provide positive encouragement to all athletes on a regular basis—*Mastery*

e. Support participants in developing themselves fully as both athletes and individuals—*Application*

f. Allow athletes time and opportunity to participate in a variety of activities outside of sport in support of a balanced lifestyle—*Application*

g. Encourage athletes to be well-educated and to become well-rounded individuals—*Awareness*

h. Recognize the connections between sport and other activities in which athletes participate—*Awareness*

Standard 23. Identify and interpret to co-coaches, athletes, concerned others and the general public the values that are to be developed from participation in sports programs.

a. Know the benefits and objectives associated with competitive athletics—*Application*

b. Communicate the benefits and objectives of athletics to others at every opportunity—*Application*

c. Understand the basic components of good sportsmanship—*Mastery*

d. Require athletes to display good sportsmanship at all times—*Mastery*

e.   Relate sportsmanship to complying with the intent of rules, not just the letter of them—*Application*

Standard 24. Identify and apply ethical conduct in sport by maintaining emotional control and demonstrating respect for athletes, officials and other coaches.

a.   Exhibit self-control and self-discipline at all times—*Application*

b.   Recognize the effect coach behavior may have on athletes, officials and spectators; provide a good role model for others—*Application*

c.   Be positive, courteous and considerate when dealing with others (athletes, officials, opponents, concerned others and spectators) in stressful situations—*Application*

d.   Know the rules of the sport coached; understand that knowledge of the rules on the part of coaches, athletes and spectators can minimize conflicts with officials and maximize performance—*Application*

e.   Know that competition requires respect and positive regard by opponents, coaching staffs, officials and spectators—that the conduct of all participants affects the quality of the sport experience for everyone—*Application*

Standard 25. Demonstrate effective motivational skills and provide positive, appropriate feedback.

a.   Recognize the importance of self-confidence and self-esteem to the athlete development—*Mastery*

b.   Enhance athletes' self-esteem by such methods as showing acceptance, reacting positively to mistakes and giving encouragement—*Mastery*

c.   Use a variety of positive instructional methods, such specific feedback and specific encouragement and constructive criticism—*Mastery*

d.   Know the social and emotional reasons for people becoming involved in athletics (among these are enjoyment, improving skills and learning new ones, the excitement of competition, being with friends and making new friends and enjoying success and recognition)—*Mastery*

Standard 26. Conduct practices and competitions to enhance the physical, social and emotional growth of athletes.

a.   Provide an appropriate model for interacting with teammates, opponents, officials and others—*Application*

b.   Emphasize the importance of enjoying practices and competitions—*Mastery*

c.   Provide opportunities for athletes to derive satisfaction from striving for personal and group goals—*Application*

d.   Use the sport experience to support positive social behaviors—such as "fair play," sportsmanship, hard work towards group goals, working as a unit, accepting responsibility for success and failure and self--—*Awareness*

e.   Develop positive social behaviors in athletes by acknowledging acts of sportsmanship, encouraging respect for teammates and opponents, respecting effort and improvement and stressing personal involvement and self-control—*Application*

f.   Structure practice and game experiences so that participants find them satisfying, positive experiences that provide an opportunity to develop the positive values associated with competition—*Application*

Standard 27. Be sufficiently familiar with the basic principles of goal setting to motivate athletes toward immediate and long range goals.

a.   Recognize the difference between short and long-range goals—*Awareness*

c.   Prepare short and long-range coaching goals—*Application*

Standard 29. Identify desirable behaviors and structure experiences to develop such behaviors in each athlete.

a.   Model desirable behaviors and use a variety of skills appropriate to specific situations—*Application*

b.   Allow all athletes to fill leadership positions at appropriate times—*Application*

c.   Identify desirable behaviors exhibited by athletes; these may include the ability to plan and organize activities, charisma, enthusiasm and the ability to help teammates perform better—*Awareness*

d.   Distinguish between positive (planning and organizing skills, enthusiasm) and negative (bullying, dictatorial) behaviors; utilize and encourage the former and avoid and discourage the latter—*Awareness*

Domain: Skills, Tactics and Strategies

Standard 30. Identify and apply specific competitive tactics and strategies appropriate for the age and skill levels involved.

a.   Know and identify both efficient and inefficient performances of the basic skills of the sport; be able to analyze and correct typical errors in performance—*Application*

b.   Know all the rules of the sport and teach them to athletes—*Application*

c.   Know the vocabulary necessary to communicate with coaches and athletes—*Application*

d.   Know the basic strategies and tactics of the sport; be able to apply them in appropriate situations—*Application*

e.   Understand that the athlete's ability to use tactics and understand strategies are developmental and that athletes must master basic ones before learning advanced strategies and tactics—*Awareness*

f.   Select strategies and tactics based upon the age, skill, experience and conditioning level of the athletes—*Application*

g.   Recognize that the performance of skills and techniques is determined by the athlete's maturity and experience—*Awareness*

Standard 31. Organize and implement materials for scouting, planning practices and analysis of games.

a.   Implement both seasonal and daily practice plans—*Application*

b.   Summarize, evaluate and maintain records of drills and practice plans used—*Application*

Standard 32. Understand and enforce the rules and regulations of appropriate bodies that govern sport and education.

a.   Know the rules and regulations (of relevant governing bodies) concerning participation in the sport—*Application*

b.   Strictly enforce the rules of the governing body—especially as they relate to athlete eligibility to participate—*Application*

c.   Properly complete all forms validating the eligibility of athletes—*Mastery*

d.   Develop and maintain a system for keeping athlete records current and secure—*Application*

Standard 33. Organize, conduct and evaluate practice sessions with regard to established program goals that are appropriate for different stages of the season.

b.   Arrange these skills and introduce them in a logical sequence; use a season planning calendar to indicate when each skill or tactic will be taught—*Application*

e.   After the competitive season, summarize and analyze successes and areas needing improvement—*Application*

Domain: Teaching and Administration

Standard 34. Know the key elements of sport principles and technical skills as well as the various teaching methods that can be used to introduce and refine them.

a.   Know the key elements of effective practice plans and prepare sample seasonal, weekly and daily plans; include a variety of activities and drills in daily plans—*Application*

b.   Know the techniques of corrective action and personnel management that are appropriate to the age of the athletes being coached—*Application*

c.   Know and apply steps for systematically instructing athletes as they progress developmentally in the skills of the sport—*Application*

d.   Demonstrate the ability to communicate effectively, using appropriate available technology—*Application*

e.   Learn and apply the elements of effective instruction—*Awareness*

Standard 35. Demonstrate objective and effective procedures for the evaluation and selection of personnel involved in the athletic program and for periodic program reviews.

a. Identify the desirable characteristics and abilities to be attained by each athlete throughout the season—*Awareness*

b. Consider the desired characteristics and abilities when preparing regular evaluations of the athletes—as they try out, during the season and at the end of the season—*Awareness*

c. Provide athletes with evaluations of personal achievement and discuss the results with each athlete individually at regular intervals—*Awareness*

d. Evaluate the effectiveness of coaching techniques used as they relate to the performance of athletes—*Application*

e. Understand that coaching effectiveness is determined by the degree to which athletes meet previously established objectives and that both peer and self-evaluation are effective tools—*Awareness*

Domain: Professional Preparation and Development

Standard 36. Demonstrate organizational and administrative efficiency in implementing sports programs, e. g. event management, budgetary procedures, facility maintenance, participation in public relations activities.

a. Organize and conduct effective meetings before, during and after the season; these meetings—for such groups as athletes, staff, guardians and alumni—can be used to prevent, solve or manage problems of the group—*Application*

b. Maintain informal, personal contacts designed to collect information and keep open lines of communication among all parties—*Mastery*

c. Use appropriate administrative forms related to (but not necessarily limited to) physical examinations for athletes, emergency procedures, injury reports, parents' meetings, program evaluation, facility scheduling, travel and budgeting—*Mastery*

d. Regularly inspect equipment and know how to arrange for repair/replacement as needed—*Mastery*

g. Recognize the need for preparing and maintaining administrative records; maintain such records; store them for the required period of time—*Awareness*

h. Demonstrate the ability to manage effectively the key elements of contests; these include inspecting and approving facilities, transportation, competitors, crowd control, locker room supervision and public relations—*Awareness*

• •

Standard 37. Acquire sufficient practical field experience and supervision in the essential coaching areas to ensure an adequate level of coaching competence for the level of sport coached. This would include a variety of knowledge, skills and experiences. The coach should:

a. Know the appropriate sequence used to teach necessary skills to developing athletes and the means for assessing the skill level and progress of athletes—*Awareness*

b. Prepare a season plan considering the abilities of in-coming athletes and maximum facilitation of their skills during the season—*Awareness*

c. Prepare practice plans that reflect reasonable time allowances for skill development in consideration of the sequential nature of skill acquisition—*Awareness*

d. Prepare written practice plans that follow guidelines for effective instruction and meeting the athlete needs—*Awareness*

e. Evaluate athletes during practice sessions; identify those who are able to enter higher levels of competition on the basis of predetermined criteria, such as skill, ability, adherence to rules and social/psychological considerations—*Awareness*

f. Assign positions, events and develop line-ups, orders and rotations that reflect the capabilities and readiness of the athletes—*Awareness*

g. Select skills and strategies appropriate to the sport and choose those that are consistent with athlete abilities—*Awareness*

h. Make appropriate coaching decisions during competition and adjust decisions based on situation—such as changes in strategy or tactics, safety considerations or competitive flow—*Awareness*

i. Teach the rules governing competition to all athletes—*Awareness*

j. Evaluate team play and individual performance in order to correct errors and facilitate maximum performance—*Awareness*

k. Evaluate player development and team play over the course of a season—*Awareness*

l. Deal effectively and sensitively with parents and guardians and/or others concerned with individual athletes—*Awareness*

m. Relate positively to officials, opposing coaches and athletes, and spectators—*Awareness*

n. Be aware of current developments in the sport through attending clinics and workshops, reading professional publications and communicating with other coaches and professionals—*Awareness*

o. Utilize guidelines for effective instruction—*Awareness*

p. Emphasize and foster self-control and self-discipline by athletes—*Awareness*

q. Evaluate effectiveness of drills—*Awareness*

r. Prepare desired outcomes for the athletic program which emphasize the growth and development of athletes—*Awareness*

s. Sequence practices so that athletes become increasingly responsible for themselves and elements of practice—*Awareness*

u. Take advantage of educational opportunities related to non-sport specific aspects of coaching—*Mastery*

Model Competencies
Level 3

Domain: Injuries: Prevention, Care and Management

Standard 1. Prevent injuries by recognizing and insisting on safe playing conditions.

g. Know that safety equipment, coach's vigilance and other safeguards provide protection against athletes over-extending themselves—*Mastery*

Standard 3. Recognize that proper conditioning and good health are vital to the prevention of athletic injuries.

a. Instruct athletes in aerobic and anaerobic conditioning programs appropriate for the sport and athletes being coached—*Mastery*

c. Know how aerobic and anaerobic energy is produced and relate these two energy systems to the demands of the sport coached—*Mastery*

d. Prepare practice plans incorporating conditioning activities designed to develop both energy systems as required by the sport; indicate which system is being developed—*Mastery*

e. Know the role played by the musculo/skeletal system in skill development and prevention of injuries—*Mastery*

g. Understand and be able to implement the different types of muscular training (interval, circuit and weight training) as they relate to sport and athletes being coached—*Mastery*

h. Know how skill instruction, conditioning, preventative care and coaching decisions influence the risk of injury to athletes—*Mastery*

i. Plan in-season and out-of-season activities designed to develop those elements of total conditioning required by the sport—*Mastery*

Standard 4. Prevent exposure to the risk of injuries by considering the effects of environmental conditions on the circulatory and respiratory systems when planning and scheduling practices and contests and implementing programs for physical conditioning.

a. Be able to describe the functioning of the circulatory and respiratory systems and how these functions react to serious stresses—*Mastery*

b. Recognize the differences of athlete response to circulatory/respiratory stress—*Application*

c. Know how such environmental factors as temperature, humidity, altitude and general climate can represent a risk to athletes and how such risk can be reduced—*Mastery*

d. Know how clothing worn for practice and competition can affect the risks associated with various environmental conditions—*Mastery*

e. Prepare practice plans that allow for dealing with dangerous environmental factors; be prepared to limit activity to reduce risk—*Mastery*

f. Provide for unlimited fluid/water intake during physical activity andinstruct athletes about proper hydration and acclemitization—*Mastery*

g. Know the most common pre-existing conditions of athletes, e.g. asthma, allergies, diabetes, improper body fat levels, nutritional deficiencies, cardiac conditions, seizures, repeated concussion, serious orthopedic injury; how to identify those athletes suffering from these conditions; the circumstances in which these conditions put the athlete at unusual risk; how to moderate activity to effectively reduce that risk; how to recognize smptoms indicating that the condition is causing the athlete to suffer activity related injury/illness; and how to appropriately respond to such indications—*Mastery*

Standard 6. Demonstrate skill in the prevention, recognition and evaluation of injuries and the ability to assist athletes with the recovery/rehabilitation from injuries that are generally associated with participation in athletics in accordance with guidelines provided by qualified medical personnel.

Prevention

c. Teach athletes to distinguish among different types of injuries and related pain (for example, sharp pain in joints that may indicate injuries that will worsen if proper rest or treatment are not provided as compared to aches within muscles which may be an acceptable element of conditioning and fitness)—*Awareness*

Management

k. Consider such factors as the type of injury, the need for reconditioning and the athlete's skill level when preparing a plan for aiding an athlete in returning from injury—*Awareness*

l. Help athletes understand how injury and subsequent recovery programs may affect their level of performance—*Application*

m. Require injured athletes to follow through with a conditioning regimen prepared by medical personnel—*Application*

n. Teach athletes that rehabilitation of injuries should be initiated under the guidance of medical personnel—*Awareness*

o. Understand the psychological consequences of injury and assist athletes in dealing with them—*Awareness*

p. Help athletes realize how such issues as "playing with pain" influence decisions about recovery programs and the time allotted to them—*Awareness*

r. Emphasize to athletes that such elements as communication with care givers and skills for coping with becoming dependent upon medical personnel are part of the recovery program—*Awareness*

Standard 7. Facilitate a unified medical program of prevention, care and management of injuries by coordinating the roles and actions of the coach and a NATA certified athletic trainer with those of the physician.

Prevention

c. Involve a NATA certified athletic trainer, exercise physiologist or physician of sports medicine in preparing a plan for conditioning athletes for specific sports—*Awareness*

d. Cooperate with qualified medical personnel to prepare a summary of season injuries and analyze the summary of season injuries to discover possible injury patterns—*Mastery*

e. Change coaching techniques *and/or conditioning programs* when injury patterns suggest a need to do so; for example, if ankle sprains were common, consider whether and how the joint can be made less susceptible through training—*Mastery*

Standard 8. Provide coaching assistants, athletes and parents/guardians with education about injury prevention, injury reporting and sources of medical care.

a. Be informed about the availability of clinics, workshops, journals, books and related resources that provide current information about injury prevention, treatment and care—*Mastery*

b. Know sources of information that can be shared with assistant coaches and parent/guardians concerning the care and treatment of injured athletes—*Mastery*

c. Encourage assistant coaches and parent/guardians to participate in educational programs that emphasize the prevention, reporting and care of injuries—*Mastery*

Domain: Risk Management

Standard 9. Understand the scope of legal responsibilities that comes with assuming a coaching position, e. g. proper supervision, planning and instruction, matching participants, safety, first aid and risk management.

g. Be able to match participants in terms of such characteristics as age, maturity, size, skill and experience; group participants appropriately—*Mastery*

Standard 12. Participate in continuing education regarding rules changes, improvements in equipment, philosophical changes, better techniques and other information in order to enhance the health, safety and success of the athlete.

b. Attend clinics, workshops and/or in-service education programs designed for coaches in order to obtain information necessary for coaching—*Mastery*

c. Read professional publications dealing with the sport coached for information on safety, proper equipment and coaching strategies—*Mastery*

d. When opportunities arise, communicate with other coaches about the sport, how it should be taught and how it can be made safer—*Mastery*

Domain: Growth, Development and Learning

Standard 13. Recognize the developmental physical changes that occur as athletes move from youth through adulthood and know how these changes influence the sequential learning and performance of motor skills in a specific sport.

a. Demonstrate knowledge of the general developmental sequence in mental, motor and physical abilities—*Application*

b. Recognize the physical and motor limitations of athletes common to the age and skill level being coached and adjust expectations accordingly—*Mastery*

c. Choose drills and practice plans which allow athletes the opportunity to improve while not forcing them to extend themselves beyond their physical and mental-emotional limits—*Mastery*

d. Teach skills and strategies that are within the performance limits of the athletes—*Mastery*

e. Recognize the developmental stages of athletes and know how they relate to *a specific* sport as either limits *to* or prerequisites for performance—*Awareness*

Standard 14. Understand the social and emotional development of the athletes being coached, know how to recognize problems related to this development and know where to refer them for appropriate assistance when necessary.

a. Recognize the typical behaviors exhibited by athletes of the age groups being coached—*Mastery*

b. Know the different general stages of social and emotional development of the athletes being coached and realize the developmental differences that may exist—*Mastery*

c. Be aware of social-psychological issues that may affect athletes of different ages in contemporary society; these may include such factors as peer pressure, lowered self-esteem, single-parent families, substance abuse, violence, sexual identity, emotional stress and child abuse—*Mastery*

d. Know how to recognize psycho-social distress and the resources available to assist athletes—*Application*

e. Refer athletes with social and emotional problems to appropriate professionals for assistance —*Awareness*

f. Know and educate athletes and parent/guardian how social psychological problems may increase susceptibility to injuries or influence recovery—*Application*

Standard 15. Analyze human performance in terms of developmental information and individual body structure.

d. Recognize that athlete performance is determined by developmental level, chronological age, experience and genetic endowment— *Mastery*

e. Recognize differences in body structures specific to the age group and sport being coached—*Awareness*

f. Know the basic movement capabilities and limitations of various body parts—*Awareness*

g. Know the limitations on physical performance of the various elements involved in the body movement—*Awareness*

h. Understand the essentials of anatomy and biomechanics as they relate to physical activity generally and specifically—*Awareness*

i. Understand how biomechanical factors can limit motor performance skills—*Awareness*

j. Establish performance goals that reflect the developmental levels of the athletes—*Awareness*

k. Know how the body type of athletes affects their performance of the needed motor skills—*Awareness*

l. Know the athlete may extend the limits of their abilities by learning to compensate for specific limitations—*Awareness*

m. Evaluate athletic performance based on possible movements and mechanical limitations of the individual athlete—*Mastery*

n. Prepare season-end evaluations of the athlete progress relative to developmental level and relevant variables in body structure— *Mastery*

o. Know which body systems and physiological factors are key to athletic performance, and apply this knowledge in designing training and practices—*Application*

Standard 16. Provide instruction to develop sport-specific motor skills. Refer athletes to appropriate counsel as needed.

a. Recognize the general developmental characteristics of the relevantathlete population and their common problems; these may include such items as problems with eye-hand coordination, visual training needs, growth spurts, maturational problems and over-use injuries—*Application*

b. Emphasize life-long activity and enjoyment of physical activity as goals of athletic participation—*Mastery*

c. Know community and medical resources are available to assist with problems affecting the athletes coached—*Awareness*

e. Know how such factors as motivation, physical development and emotional maturity influence the ability of athletes to learn new skills—*Application*

f. Aid athletes in assessing their own abilities accurately —*Application*

g. Know the over-all requirements and opportunities of the relevant sport so that athletes can be made aware of opportunities open to them—*Awareness*

h. Find additional opportunities in the sport for those participants who are highly motivated or particularly capable of higher levels of achievement—*Awareness*

Standard 17. Provide learning experiences appropriate to the growth and development of the age group coached.

a. Acquire or prepare season objectives that reflect the physical and motor development of the athletes—*Mastery*

b. Select specific drills and activities that allow athletes of various levels to experience success—*Mastery*

c. Use a variety of activities to help athletes of various levels of ability develop specific skills—*Application*

Domain: Training, Conditioning and Nutrition

Standard 18. Demonstrate a basic knowledge of physiological systems and their responses to training and conditioning.

a. Know the five essentials of conditioning: Warm up/cool down, overload, progression, specificity and reversibility; implement them according to the developmental level of the athletes—*Mastery*

b. Know the components of the physiological systems involved with athletic conditioning—*Mastery*

c. Know how the cardiovascular and muscular systems produce energy and how they respond to training—*Mastery*

d. Understand muscular strength, power, endurance and flexibility; know how each is required of athletes; implement training programs that develop these elements based on the developmental maturity of the athletes—*Mastery*

e. Know common methods of conditioning (such as interval, circuit and weight training) and use each appropriately in preparing a complete conditioning program for athletes—*Application*

f. Prepare a comprehensive plan for both in-season and out-of-season conditioning of athletes—*Application*

g. Considering the sport being coached and individual differences of athletes, apply the principles of conditioning to the needs of athletes—*Awareness*

Standard 19. Design programs of training and conditioning that properly incorporate the mechanics of movement and sound physiological principles taking into account each individual's ability and medical history, avoiding contraindicated exercises and activities and guarding against the possibility of over-training; be able to modify programs as needed.

c. Know the components of physical fitness and the appropriate levels of each in relation to age and sport-specific demands—*Mastery*

d. Assess the existing sport-specific fitness levelsof the athletes—*Awareness*

e. Know how the age, development and needs of athletes determine the appropriate levels of training and conditioning—*Awareness*

f. Identify and use activities that simultaneously provide for more than one area of conditioning—*Application*

g. Prepare practice plans that train and condition the entire group while creating opportunities for individual athletes to meet specific needs—*Application*

h. Distinguish between minimal and advanced levels of training and conditioning; be able to implement each according to the athlete needs—*Application*

i. Assess the level of development and interest shown by the athletes for involvement in appropriate off-season conditioning programs—*Awareness*

j. Implement training programs that can be placed in a developmental sequence appropriate for the highly-motivated athlete—*Application*

k. Know the indicators of overtraining (i.e. lack of interest in practice, lowered levels of performance, minor injuries failing to heal or chronic complaining about practice or injury); regularly assess the athletes coached for these indicators—*Awareness*

l. Know techniques to mediate/reduce of over-training (i.e. increased variety of drills/activities allowing athletes to organize practices, shortening practice sessions and practicing at different times or in different settings) to reduce or eliminate these symptoms—*Awareness*

Standard 20. Demonstrate knowledge of proper nutrition and educate athletes about the effects of nutrition upon health and physical performance.

a. Know the essential food groups and how to provide a balanced diet for athletes—*Mastery*

b. Know what foods to suggest for a pre-competition meal and when this meal should be eaten—*Mastery*

c. Know the effects on performance of using pharmacological aids such as steroids, amphetamines and caffeine—*Awareness*

d. Understand the demands of athletics as they relate to increased or specialized dietary needs—*Application*

e. Know whether dietary supplements are necessary or desirable for athletes—*Mastery*

f. Understand the issues of body composition and weight control and recognize signs of eating disorders—*Awareness*

g. Refer athletes with nutritional problems (such as weight control or use of performance enhancing substances) for appropriate professional assistance—*Awareness*

Standard 21. Demonstrate knowledge of the use and abuse of drugs and promote sound chemical health.

a. Demonstrate/model appropriate behavior regarding sound chemical health. Show concern for the use and abuse of chemicals by athletes and be prepared to intervene—*Mastery*

b. Recognize typical drug use patterns exhibited by athletes and intervene if necessary—*Application*

c. Know the legal responsibilities of adults working with minors as they relate to potential use of alcohol, tobacco and other drugs—*Mastery*

d. Know how the use and abuse of chemicals affects athletic performance—*Application*

e. Understand the social, emotional and psychological pressures placed upon athletes which make them susceptible to drug use—*Application*

f. Plan/facilitate participation by drug free athletes—*Application*

g. Know and use appropriate agencies to provide assistance in prevention and treatment of drug use—*Mastery*

h. Know how the side-effects of medically prescribed drugs and medications may affect athletic performance—*Application*

Domain: Social/psychological Aspects of Coaching

Standard 22. Subscribe to a philosophy that acknowledges the role of athletics in developing the complete person.

a. Recognize that each athlete is an individual with unique needs and treat athletes accordingly—*Mastery*

b. Organize activities so that athletes have an opportunity to develop/maintain positive feelings of self-worth—*Mastery*

e. Support participants in developing themselves fully as both athletes and individuals—*Mastery*

f. Allow athletes time and opportunity to participate in a variety of activities outside of sport in support of a balanced lifestyle—*Mastery*

g. Encourage athletes to be well-educated and to become well-rounded individuals—*Mastery*

h. Recognize the connections between sport and other activities in which athletes participate—*Mastery*

i. Assist athletes in learning to manage time appropriately—*Application*

j. Identify the ideas and principles guiding your coaching efforts to reflect a concern for the emotional and physical health of your athletes—*Application*

Standard 23. Identify and interpret to co-coaches, athletes, concerned others and the general public the values that are to be developed from participation in sports programs.

a. Know the benefits and objectives associated with competitive athletics—*Mastery*

b. Communicate the benefits and objectives of athletics to others at every opportunity—*Mastery*

e. Relate sportsmanship to complying with the intent of rules, not just the letter of them—*Mastery*

f. Regularly discuss with athletes both actual and hypothetical situations involving ethics in a sport setting—*Awareness*

g. Relate to athletes instances in which ethical conduct translates from sport to life in general—*Awareness*

Standard 24. Identify and apply ethical conduct in sport by maintaining emotional control and demonstrating respect for athletes, officials and other coaches.

a. Exhibit self-control and self-discipline at all times—*Mastery*

b. Recognize the effect coach behavior may have on athletes, officials and spectators; provide a good role model for others—*Mastery*

c. Be positive, courteous and considerate when dealing with others (athletes, officials, opponents, concerned others and spectators) in stressful situations—*Mastery*

d. Know the rules of the sport coached; understand that knowledge of the rules on the part of coaches, athletes and spectators can minimize conflicts with officials and maximize performance—*Mastery*

e. Know that competition requires respect and positive regard by opponents, coaching staffs, officials and spectators—that the conduct of all participants affects the quality of the sport experience for everyone—*Mastery*

f. Learn stress management techniques such as progressive relaxation, deep breathing, behavior modeling, visualization and positive self-talk and be able to teach them to the athletes; assist athletes in using these techniques to deal with competitive stress—*Awareness*

g. Use stress management skills to defuse potentially difficult emotional situations—*Awareness*

Standard 25. Demonstrate effective motivational skills and provide positive, appropriate feedback.

e. Know and use appropriate goal-setting strategies, alternative goals, individual support, arousal techniques, etc.; the positive approach to correcting errors and the questionable function of inspirational speeches as ways of reducing the athletes' fear of failure and so reducing the level of stress felt in practice and competition—*Application*

Standard 26. Conduct practices and competitions to enhance the physical, social and emotional growth of athletes.

a. Provide an appropriate model for interacting with teammates, opponents, officials and others—*Mastery*

c. Provide opportunities for athletes to derive satisfaction from striving for personal and group goals—*Mastery*

d. Use the sport experience to support positive social behaviors—such as "fair play," sportsmanship, hard work towards group goals, working as a unit, accepting responsibility for success and failure and self-—*Mastery*

e. Develop positive social behaviors in athletes by acknowledging acts of sportsmanship, encouraging respect for teammates and opponents, respecting effort and improvement and stressing personal involvement and self-control—*Mastery*

f. Structure practice and game experiences so that participants find them satisfying, positive experiences that provide an opportunity to develop the positive values associated with competition—*Mastery*

Standard 27. Be sufficiently familiar with the basic principles of goal setting to motivate athletes toward immediate and long range goals.

a. Recognize the difference between short and long-range goals—*Mastery*

b. Help athletes prepare short and long-range goals for themselves and their team, recognizing that goal setting can have both positive and negative consequences—*Awareness*

c. Prepare short and long-range coaching goals—*Mastery*

d. Assist athletes in relating long-range goals for participation to the realities of competition and the need to develop non-sports related interests and talents—*Awareness*

Standard 28. Treat each athlete as an individual while recognizing the dynamic relationship of personality and socio-cultural variables such as gender, race and socio-economic differences.

a. Recognize that social environment influences the behaviors and personalities of athletes—*Awareness*

b. Understand how social, cultural and emotional forces interact in creating athlete personalities—*Awareness*

c. Understand the many dimensions of personality that may be expressed in athletics and teach athletes how to deal with these differences—*Awareness*

d. Accept differences in personality as another necessary component in preparing athletes for competition—*Awareness*

Standard 29. Identify desirable behaviors and structure experiences to develop such behaviors in each athlete.

a. Model desirable behaviors and use a variety of skills appropriate to specific situations—*Mastery*

b. Allow all athletes to fill leadership positions at appropriate times—*Mastery*

c. Identify desirable behaviors exhibited by athletes; these may include the ability to plan and organize activities, charisma, enthusiasm and the ability to help teammates perform better—*Application*

d. Distinguish between positive (planning and organizing skills, enthusiasm) and negative (bullying, dictatorial) behaviors; utilize and encourage the former and avoid and discourage the latter—*Mastery*

e. Prepare practice and season plans that establish and reinforce the development of desirable behavior for all athletes—*Application*

Domain: Skills, Tactics and Strategies

Standard 30. Identify and apply specific competitive tactics and strategies appropriate for the age and skill levels involved.

a. Know and identify both efficient and inefficient performances of the basic skills of the sport; be able to analyze and correct typical errors in performance—*Mastery*

b. Know all the rules of the sport and teach them to athletes—*Mastery*

c. Know the vocabulary necessary to communicate with coaches and athletes—*Mastery*

d. Know the basic strategies and tactics of the sport; be able to apply them in appropriate situations—*Mastery*

e. Understand that the athlete's ability to use tactics and understand strategies are developmental and that athletes must master basic ones before learning advanced strategies and tactics—*Application*

f. Select strategies and tactics based upon the age, skill, experience and conditioning level of the athletes—*Mastery*

g. Recognize that the performance of skills and techniques is determined by the athlete's maturity and experience—*Mastery*

h. Prepare situationally-specific plans that reflect the abilities of the athletes—*Awareness*

i. Prepare end-of-contest and special situation strategies for use as needed—*Application*

j. Understand how rules may dictate strategy, and be able to implement appropriate strategies in competitive situations—*Awareness*

Standard 31. Organize and implement materials for scouting, planning practices and analysis of games.

a. Implement both seasonal and daily practice plans—*Mastery*

b. Summarize, evaluate and maintain records of drills and practice plans used—*Mastery*

c. Recognize the necessity of scouting opponents at upper levels of play in many sports—*Awareness*

d. Be able to scout opponents, assess and analyze strengths and weaknesses, and document information in a usable form—*Awareness*

e. Demonstrate the ability to develop a competition plan based on assessment of opponents and the athlete's abilities—*Application*

f. Prepare a written game plan summary that considers opponent tendencies and identifies strategies and tactics for positive results—*Awareness*

g. Develop and use meaningful aids for analysis of competitions; these should include such information as individual and team statistics, videotapes and assessments by observers—*Application*

h. Be able to anticipate the likely strategies of opposing coaches and be prepared to respond to them in a timely manner—*Awareness*

Standard 32. Understand and enforce the rules and regulations of appropriate bodies that govern sport and education.

a. Know the rules and regulations (of relevant governing bodies) concerning participation in the sport—*Mastery*

b. Strictly enforce the rules of the governing body—especially as they relate to athlete eligibility to participate—*Mastery*

d. Develop and maintain a system for keeping athlete records current and secure—*Mastery*

Standard 33. Organize, conduct and evaluate practice sessions with regard to established program goals that are appropriate for different stages of the season.

a. Determine which skills in each area of the sport experience—physical skills, knowledge of the sport, physical fitness and personal/social skills—are to be taught at each level within the total program—*Mastery*

b. Arrange these skills and introduce them in a logical sequence; use a season planning calendar to indicate when each skill or tactic will be taught—*Mastery*

c. Teach the skills and tactics through practice activities that reflect competitive experiences—*Awareness*

d. Stress performance as the measure of progress in learning skills—*Awareness*

e. After the competitive season, summarize and analyze successes and areas needing improvement—*Mastery*

f. Use season analysis and summary along with the seasonal and individual practice schedules to assist in planning for the succeeding season—*Awareness*

g. Evaluate the progress of individual athletes in achieving pre-determined goals—*Awareness*

h. Consult with experienced coaches and educators for aid in assessing the athlete progress—*Awareness*

Domain: Teaching and Administration

Standard 34. Know the key elements of sport principles and technical skills as well as the various teaching methods that can be used to introduce and refine them.

a. Know the key elements of effective practice plans and prepare sample seasonal, weekly and daily plans; include a variety of activities and drills in daily plans—*Application*

b. Know the techniques of corrective action and personnel management that are appropriate to the age of the athletes being coached—*Mastery*

c. Know and apply steps for systematically instructing athletes as they progress developmentally in the skills of the sport—*Application*

d. Demonstrate the ability to communicate effectively, using appropriate available technology—*Mastery*

e. Learn and apply the elements of effective instruction—*Mastery*

f. Prepare a set of desired outcomes for the sport coached; these should emphasize athlete growth and development—*Application*

g. Sequence practices so that all athletes develop a sense of self-control and discipline as they become increasingly responsible for themselves and elements of practice—*Mastery*

h. Evaluate drills based on their effectiveness in developing skills and tactics appropriate for the level of competition—*Mastery*

Standard 35. Demonstrate objective and effective procedures for the evaluation and selection of personnel involved in the athletic program and for periodic program reviews.

a. Identify the desirable characteristics and abilities to be attained by each athlete throughout the season—*Mastery*

b. Consider the desired characteristics and abilities when preparing regular evaluations of the athletes—as they try out, during the season and at the end of the season—*Mastery*

c. Provide athletes with evaluations of personal achievement and discuss the results with each athlete individually at regular intervals—*Mastery*

d. Evaluate the effectiveness of coaching techniques used as they relate to the performance of athletes—*Mastery*

e. Understand that coaching effectiveness is determined by the degree to which athletes meet previously established objectives and that both peer and self-evaluation are effective tools—*Mastery*

f. Follow an established sequence for evaluation which involves the identification of objectives, data collection, analysis of data and making the needed changes—*Application*

g. Record data about athlete performance (such as a checklist of effective coaching actions and records of progress by the athletes) in order to monitor progress and coaching effectiveness—*Application*

h. Establish criteria for the selection and elimination of members of a team or squad; apply these criteria with fairness and integrity—*Application*

i. Prepare job descriptions for assistants, managers, team captains, etc.—*Awareness*

j. Prepare a list of performance objectives for additional personnel—*Awareness*

k. Evaluate program personnel—including assistant coaches, managers and trainers—*Awareness*

l. Use formal, written evaluations to assist in selecting and retaining program personnel—*Awareness*

m. Know and be able to implement diplomatic, sensitive ways in which to communicate with program personnel—athletes trying out, players, co-coaches and others—about their status and performance—*Application*

Domain: Professional Preparation and Development

Standard 36. Demonstrate organizational and administrative efficiency in implementing sports programs, e. g. event management, budgetary procedures, facility maintenance, participation in public relations activities.

a. Organize and conduct effective meetings before, during and after the season; these meetings—for such groups as athletes, staff, guardians and alumni—can be used to prevent, solve or manage problems of the group—*Mastery*

e. Establish record keeping procedures to account for sports equipment and its maintenance—*Application*

f. Be involved in public relations activities within both the sport and the community—*Awareness*

g. Recognize the need for preparing and maintaining administrative records; maintain such records; store them for the required period of time—*Mastery*

h. Demonstrate the ability to manage the key elements of contests; these include inspecting and approving facilities, transportation, competitors, crowd control, locker room supervision and public relations—*Application*

i. Develop and maintain a record keeping system for administrative forms and correspondence—*Application*

Standard 37. Acquire sufficient practical field experience and supervision in the essential coaching areas to ensure an adequate level of coaching competence for the level of sport coached. This would include a variety of knowledge, skills and experiences. The coach should:

a. Know the appropriate sequence used to teach necessary skills to developing athletes and the means for assessing the skill level and progress of athletes—*Application*

b. Prepare a season plan considering the abilities of in-coming athletes and maximum facilitation of their skills during the season—*Application*

c. Prepare practice plans that reflect reasonable time allowances for skill development in consideration of the sequential nature of skill acquisition—*Application*

d. Prepare written practice plans that follow guidelines for effective instruction and meeting the athlete needs—*Application*

e. Evaluate athletes during practice sessions; identify those who are able to enter higher levels of competition on the basis of predetermined criteria, such as skill, ability, adherence to rules and social/psychological considerations—*Application*

f. Assign positions, events and develop line-ups, orders and rotations that reflect the capabilities and readiness of the athletes—*Application*

g. Select skills and strategies appropriate to the sport and choose those that are consistent with athlete abilities—*Application*

h. Make appropriate coaching decisions during competition and adjust decisions based on situation—such as changes in strategy or tactics, safety considerations or competitive flow—*Application*

i. Teach the rules governing competition to all athletes—*Applicaiton*

j. Evaluate team play and individual performance in order to correct errors and facilitate maximum performance—*Application*

k. Evaluate player development and team play over the course of a season—*Application*

l. Deal effectively and sensitively with parents and guardians and/or others concerned with individual athletes—*Application*

m. Relate positively to officials, opposing coaches and athletes, and spectators—*Application*

n. Be aware of current developments in the sport through attending clinics and workshops, reading professional publications and communicating with other coaches and professionals—*Application*

o. Utilize guidelines for effective instruction—*Application*

p. Emphasize and foster self-control and self-discipline by athletes—*Application*

q. Evaluate effectiveness of drills—*Application*

r. Prepare desired outcomes for the athletic program which emphasize the growth and development of athletes—*Application*

s. Sequence practices so that athletes become increasingly responsible for themselves and elements of practice—*Application*

t. Demonstrate the ability to communicate effectively using audio-visual resources—*Application*

v. At regular intervals, seek feedback from experienced coaches or assistants to evaluate practice sessions; discuss their observations and implement changes—*Awareness*

w. Scout opponents and use the information for planning contests as appropriate—*Application*

x. Apply scientific and experiential information to the improvement of the specific sport—*Awareness*

y. Participate in appropriate professional sport or coaching organizations at the local, state, regional and national levels—*Application*

z. Know the techniques for re-teaching and the motivational problems associated with re-teaching—*Awareness*

aa. Incorporate assessment and re-teaching into practices and competitions—*Awareness*

Model Competencies
Level 4

Domain: Injuries: Prevention, Care and Management

Standard 1. Prevent injuries by recognizing and insisting on safe playing conditions.

h.   Be active at your level of coaching in working for the formulation of rules that influence the safety and healthful participation of athletes in the sport coached—*Mastery*

Standard 3. Recognize that proper conditioning and good health are vital to the prevention of athletic injuries.

j.   Instruct athletes about off-season programs that will assist in maintaining appropriate levels of general fitness for sport—*Mastery*

Standard 4. Prevent exposure to the risk of injuries by considering the effects of environmental conditions on the circulatory and respiratory systems when planning and scheduling practices and contests and implementing programs for physical conditioning.

b.   Recognize the differences of athlete response to circulatory/respiratory stress—*Mastery*

Standard 6. Demonstrate skill in the prevention, recognition and evaluation of injuries and the ability to assist athletes with the recovery/rehabilitation from injuries that are generally associated with participation in athletics in accordance with guidelines provided by qualified medical personnel.

Prevention

c.   Teach athletes to distinguish among different types of injuries and related pain (for example, sharp pain in joints that may indicate injuries that will worsen if proper rest or treatment are not provided as compared to aches within muscles which may be an acceptable element of conditioning and fitness)—*Mastery*

Management

k.   Consider such factors as the type of injury, the need for reconditioning and the athlete's skill level when preparing a plan for aiding an athlete in returning from injury—*Mastery*

l.   Help athletes understand how injury and subsequent recovery programs may affect their level of performance—*Mastery*

m. Require injured athletes to follow through with a conditioning regimen prepared by medical personnel—*Mastery*

n.   Teach athletes that rehabilitation of injuries should be initiated under the guidance of medical personnel—*Application*

o.   Understand the psychological consequences of injury and assist athletes in dealing with them—*Mastery*

p.   Help athletes realize how such issues as "playing with pain" influence decisions about recovery programs and the time allotted to them—*Application*

r.   Emphasize to athletes that such elements as communication with care givers and skills for coping with becoming dependent upon medical personnel are part of the recovery program—*Application*

Standard 7. Facilitate a unified medical program of prevention, care and management of injuries by coordinating the roles and actions of the coach and a NATA certified athletic trainer with those of the physician.

Prevention

c.   Involve a NATA certified athletic trainer, exercise physiologist or physician of sports medicine in preparing a plan for conditioning athletes for specific sports—*Mastery*

Standard 8. Provide coaching assistants, athletes and parents/guardians with education about injury prevention, injury reporting and sources of medical care.

d.   Become involved in formulating, publicizing, interpreting and teaching policies and procedures for safe and healthful athletic participation—*Mastery*

Domain: Growth, Development and Learning

Standard 13. Recognize the developmental physical changes that occur as athletes move from youth through adulthood and know how these changes influence the sequential learning and performance of motor skills in a specific sport.

a.   Demonstrate knowledge of the general developmental sequence in mental, motor and physical abilities—*Mastery*

e.   Recognize the developmental stages of athletes and know how they relate to *a specific* sport as either limits *to* or prerequisites for performance—*Mastery*

Standard 14. Understand the social and emotional development of the athletes being coached, know how to recognize problems related to this develop-

ment and know where to refer them for appropriate assistance when necessary.

d. Know how to recognize psycho-social distress and the resources available to assist athletes—*Mastery*

e. Refer athletes with social and emotional problems to appropriate professionals for assistance —*Mastery*

f. Know and educate athletes and parent/guardian how social psychological problems may increase susceptibility to injuries or influence recovery—*Mastery*

Standard 15. Analyze human performance in terms of developmental information and individual body structure.

e. Recognize differences in body structures specific to the age group and sport being coached—*Mastery*

f. Know the basic movement capabilities and limitations of various body parts—*Mastery*

g. Know the limitations on physical performance of the various elements involved in the body movement—*Mastery*

h. Understand the essentials of anatomy and biomechanics as they relate to physical activity generally and specifically—*Mastery*

i. Understand how biomechanical factors can limit motor performance skills—*Application*

j. Establish performance goals that reflect the developmental levels of the athletes—*Application*

k. Know how the body type of athletes affects their performance of the needed motor skills—*Application*

l. Know the athlete may extend the limits of their abilities by learning to compensate for specific limitations—*Application*

o. Know which body systems and physiological factors are key to athletic performance, and apply this knowledge in designing training and practices—*Mastery*

Standard 16. Provide instruction to develop sport-specific motor skills. Refer athletes to appropriate counsel as needed.

a. Recognize the general developmental characteristics of the relevant athlete population and their common problems; these may include such items as problems with eye-hand coordination, visual training needs, growth spurts, maturational problems and over-use injuries—*Mastery*

c. Know community and medical resources are available to assist with problems affecting the athletes coached—*Mastery*

e. Know how such factors as motivation, physical development and emotional maturity influence the ability of athletes to learn new skills—*Mastery*

f. Aid athletes in assessing their own abilities accurately —*Mastery*

g. Know the over-all requirements and opportunities of the relevant sport so that athletes can be made aware of opportunities open to them—*Mastery*

h. Find additional opportunities in the sport for those participants who are highly motivated or particularly capable of higher levels of achievement—*Mastery*

Standard 17. Provide learning experiences appropriate to the growth and development of the age group coached.

c. Use a variety of activities to help athletes of various levels of ability develop specific skills—*Mastery*

Domain: Training, Conditioning and Nutrition

Standard 18. Demonstrate a basic knowledge of physiological systems and their responses to training and conditioning.

e. Know common methods of conditioning (such as interval, circuit and weight training) and use each appropriately in preparing a complete conditioning program for athletes—*Mastery*

f. Prepare a comprehensive plan for both in-season and out-of-season conditioning of athletes—*Mastery*

g. Considering the sport being coached and individual differences of athletes, apply the principles of conditioning to the needs of athletes—*Application*

Standard 19. Design programs of training and conditioning that properly incorporate the mechanics of movement and sound physiological principles taking into account each individual's ability and medical history, avoiding contraindicated exercises and activities and guarding against the possibility of over-training; be able to modify programs as needed.

d. Assess the existing sport-specific fitness levelsof the athletes—*Application*

e. Know how the age, development and needs of athletes determine the appropriate levels of training and conditioning—*Mastery*

f. Identify and use activities that simultaneously provide for more than one area of conditioning—*Mastery*

g. Prepare practice plans that train and condition the entire group while creating opportunities for individual athletes to meet specific needs—*Mastery*

h. Distinguish between minimal and advanced levels of training and conditioning; be able to implement each according to the athlete needs—*Mastery*

i. Assess the level of development and interest shown by the athletes for involvement in appropriate off-season conditioning programs—*Mastery*

j. Implement training programs that can be placed in a developmental sequence appropriate for the highly-motivated athlete—*Mastery*

k. Know the indicators of overtraining (i.e. lack of interest in practice, lowered levels of performance, minor injuries failing to heal or chronic complaining about practice or injury); regularly assess the athletes coached for these indicators—*Application*

l. Know techniques to mediate/reduce of over-training (i.e. increased variety of drills/activities allowing athletes to organize practices, shortening practice sessions and practicing at different times or in different settings) to reduce or eliminate these symptoms—*Application*

m. Know how to prevent over-training; these may include such things as cross-training, periodization and increased autonomy—*Application*

Standard 20. Demonstrate knowledge of proper nutrition and educate athletes about the effects of nutrition upon health and physical performance.

c. Know the effects on performance of using pharmacological aids such as steroids, amphetamines and caffeine—*Mastery*

d. Understand the demands of athletics as they relate to increased or specialized dietary needs—*Mastery*

f. Understand the issues of body composition and weight control and recognize signs of eating disorders—*Mastery*

g. Refer athletes with nutritional problems (such as weight control or use of performance enhancing substances) for appropriate professional assistance—*Mastery*

Standard 21. Demonstrate knowledge of the use and abuse of drugs and promote sound chemical health.

b. Recognize typical drug use patterns exhibited by athletes and intervene if necessary—*Mastery*

d. Know how the use and abuse of chemicals affects athletic performance—*Mastery*

e. Understand the social, emotional and psychological pressures placed upon athletes which make them susceptible to drug use—*Mastery*

f. Plan/facilitate participation by drug free athletes—*Mastery*

h. Know how the side-effects of medically prescribed drugs and medications may affect athletic performance—*Mastery*

Domain: Social/psychological Aspects of Coaching

Standard 22. Subscribe to a philosophy that acknowledges the role of athletics in developing the complete person.

i. Assist athletes in learning to manage time appropriately—*Mastery*

j. Identify the ideas and principles guiding your coaching efforts to reflect a concern for the emotional and physical health of your athletes—*Mastery*

Standard 23. Identify and interpret to co-coaches, athletes, concerned others and the general public the values that are to be developed from participation in sports programs.

f. Regularly discuss with athletes both actual and hypothetical situations involving ethics in a sport setting—*Mastery*

g. Relate to athletes instances in which ethical conduct translates from sport to life in general—*Application*

h. Prepare athletes to deal with media representatives; teach athletes how to interact with persons representing the media in discussions of such issues as evaluation of competition and career objectives—*Application*

Standard 24. Identify and apply ethical conduct in sport by maintaining emotional control and demonstrating respect for athletes, officials and other coaches.

f. Learn stress management techniques such as progressive relaxation, deep breathing, behavior modeling, visualization and positive self-talk and be able to teach them to the athletes; assist athletes in using these techniques to deal with competitive stress—*Application*

g. Use stress management skills to defuse potentially difficult emotional situations—*Application*

Standard 25. Demonstrate effective motivational skills and provide positive, appropriate feedback.

e. Know and use appropriate goal-setting strategies, alternative goals, individual support, arousal techniques, etc.; the positive approach to correcting errors and the questionable function of inspirational speeches as ways of reducing the athletes' fear of failure and so reducing the level of stress felt in practice and competition—*Mastery*

Standard 27. Be sufficiently familiar with the basic principles of goal setting to motivate athletes toward immediate and long range goals.

b. Help athletes prepare short and long-range goals for themselves and their team, recognizing that goal setting can have both positive and negative consequences—*Mastery*

d. Assist athletes in relating long-range goals for participation to the realities of competition and the need to develop non-sports related interests and talents on the part of everyone involved—*Application*

Standard 28. Treat each athlete as an individual while recognizing the dynamic relationship of personality and socio-cultural variables such as gender, race and socio-economic differences.

a. Recognize that social environment influences the behaviors and personalities of athletes—*Application*

b. Understand how social, cultural and emotional forces interact in creating athlete personalities—*Application*

c. Understand the many dimensions of personality that may be expressed in athletics and teach athletes how to deal with these differences—*Application*

d. Accept differences in personality as another necessary component in preparing athletes for competition—*Application*

e. Promote the equality of opportunity within the sport by encouraging participation regardless of race, gender, socio-economic status or culture; this may involve working to overcome such barriers as tradition, bias, public image, funding, regulations, policies and apathy—*Mastery*

Standard 29. Identify desirable behaviors and structure experiences to develop such behaviors in each athlete.

c. Identify *desirable behaviors* exhibited by athletes; these may include the ability to plan and organize activities, charisma, enthusiasm and the ability to help teammates perform better—*Mastery*

e. Prepare practice and season plans that establish and reinforce the development of desirable behavior for all athletes—*Mastery*

Domain: Skills, Tactics and Strategies

Standard 30. Identify and apply specific competitive tactics and strategies appropriate for the age and skill levels involved.

e. Understand that the athletes' ability to use tactics and understand strategies are developmental and that athletes must master basic ones before learning advanced strategies and tactics—*Mastery*

h. Prepare situationally-specific plans that reflect the abilities of the athletes—*Mastery*

i. Prepare end-of-contest and special situationstrategies for use as needed—*Mastery*

j. Understand how rules may dictate strategy, and be able to implement appropriate strategies in competitive situations—*Application*

Standard 31. Organize and implement materials for scouting, planning practices and analysis of games.

c. Recognize the necessity of scouting opponents at upper levels of play in many sports—*Mastery*

d. Be able to scout opponents, assess and analyze strengths and weaknesses, and document information in a usable form—*Mastery*

e. Demonstrate the ability to develop a competition plan based on assessment of opponents and the athlete's abilities—*Mastery*

f. Prepare a written game plan summary that considers opponent tendencies and identifies strategies and tactics for positive results—*Mastery*

g. Develop and use meaningful aids for analysis of competitions; these should include such information as individual and team statistics, videotapes and assessments by observers—*Mastery*

h. Be able to anticipate the likely strategies of opposing coaches and be prepared to respond to them in a timely manner—*Application*

i. Be able to identify the basic philosophy guiding the play of opponents—*Awareness*

j. Use knowledge of the opponent strategies, tactics and philosophy to aid in the preparation of game plans and the selection of strategies and tactics—*Awareness*

Standard 33. Organize, conduct and evaluate practice sessions with regard to established program goals that are appropriate for different stages of the season.

c. Teach the skills and tactics through practice activities that reflect competitive experiences—*Application*

d. Stress performance as the measure of progress in learning skills—*Application*

f. Use season analysis and summary along with the seasonal and individual practice schedules to assist in planning for the succeeding season—*Application*

g. Evaluate the progress of individual athletes in achieving pre-determined goals—*Application*

h. Consult with experienced coaches and educators for aid in assessing the athlete progress—*Application*

Domain: Teaching and Administration

Standard 34. Know the key elements of sport principles and technical skills as well as the various teaching methods that can be used to introduce and refine them.

c. Know and apply steps for systematically instructing athletes as they progress developmentally in the skills of the sport—*Mastery*

f. Prepare a set of desired outcomes for the sport coached; these should emphasize athlete growth and development—*Mastery*

i. Determine when it is necessary to re-instruct athletes in such elements as skills, strategies and rules—*Awareness*

j. Know and use the most effective instructional techniques of re-teaching—*Application*

k. Know and use different motivational techniques and reward systems in preparing athletes for sessions involving re-instruction and review—*Application*

l. Use appropriate tools such as videotapes to analyze skills and to monitor skills in both practice and competition settings—*Application*

m. Use assessment during practice to guide instruction and re-instruction—*Application*

Standard 35. Demonstrate objective and effective procedures for the evaluation and selection of personnel involved in the athletic program and for periodic program reviews.

f.   Follow an established sequence for evaluation which involves the identification of objectives, data collection, analysis of data and making the needed changes—*Mastery*

g.   Record data about athlete performance (such as a checklist of effective coaching actions and records of progress by the athletes) in order to monitor progress and coaching effectiveness—*Mastery*

h.   Establish criteria for the selection and elimination of members of a team or squad; apply these criteria with fairness and integrity—*Mastery*

i.   Prepare job descriptions for assistants, managers, team captains, etc.—*Mastery*

j.   Prepare a list of performance objectives for additional personnel—*Application*

k.   Evaluate program personnel—including assistant coaches, managers and trainers—*Mastery*

l.   Use formal, written evaluations to assist in selecting and retaining program personnel—*Application*

m.   Know and be able to implement diplomatic, sensitive ways in which to communicate with program personnel—athletes trying out, players, co-coaches and others—about their status and performance—*Mastery*

Domain: Professional Preparation and Development

Standard 36. Demonstrate organizational and administrative efficiency in implementing sports programs, e. g. event management, budgetary procedures, facility maintenance, participation in public relations activities.

e.   Establish record keeping procedures to account for sports equipment and its maintenance—*Mastery*

f.   Be involved in public relations activities within both the sport and the community—*Mastery*

h.   Demonstrate the ability to manage the key elements of contests; these include inspecting and approving facilities, transportation, competitors, crowd control, locker room supervision and public relations—*Mastery*

i.   Develop and maintain a record keeping system for administrative forms and correspondence—*Mastery*

Standard 37. Acquire sufficient practical field experience and supervision in the essential coaching areas to ensure an adequate level of coaching competence for the level of sport coached. This would include a variety of knowledge, skills and experiences. The coach should:

a. Know the appropriate sequence used to teach necessary skills to developing athletes and the means for assessing the skill level and progress of athletes—*Application*

b. Prepare a season plan considering the abilities of in-coming athletes and maximum facilitation of their skills during the season—*Application*

c. Prepare practice plans that reflect reasonable time allowances for skill development in consideration of the sequential nature of skill acquisition—*Application*

d. Prepare written practice plans that follow guidelines for effective instruction and meeting the athlete needs—*Application*

e. Evaluate athletes during practice sessions; identify those who are able to enter higher levels of competition on the basis of predetermined criteria, such as skill, ability, adherence to rules and social/psychological considerations—*Application*

f. Assign positions, events and develop line-ups, orders and rotations that reflect the capabilities and readiness of the athletes—*Application*

g. Select skills and strategies appropriate to the sport and choose those that are consistent with athlete abilities—*Application*

h. Make appropriate coaching decisions during competition and adjust decisions based on situation—such as changes in strategy or tactics, safety considerations or competitive flow—*Applicaiton*

i. Teach the rules governing competition to all athletes—*Application*

j. Evaluate team play and individual performance in order to correct errors and facilitate maximum performance—*Application*

k. Evaluate player development and team play over the course of a season—*Application*

l. Deal effectively and sensitively with parents and guardians and/or others concerned with individual athletes—*Application*

m. Relate positively to officials, opposing coaches and athletes, and spectators—*Application*

n. Be aware of current developments in the sport through attending clinics and workshops, reading professional publications and communicating with other coaches and professionals—*Application*

o. Utilize guidelines for effective instruction—*Application*

p. Emphasize and foster self-control and self-discipline by athletes—*Application*

q. Evaluate effectiveness of drills—*Application*

r. Prepare desired outcomes for the athletic program which emphasize the growth and development of athletes—*Application*

s. Sequence practices so that athletes become increasingly responsible for themselves and elements of practice—*Application*

t. Demonstrate the ability to communicate effectively using audio-visual resources—*Application*

v. At regular intervals, seek feedback from experienced coaches or assistants to evaluate practice sessions; discuss their observations and implement changes—*Application*

w. Scout opponents and use the information for planning contests as appropriate—*Mastery*

x. Apply scientific and experiential information to the improvement of the specific sport—*Application*

y. Participate in appropriate professional sport or coaching organizations at the local, state, regional and national levels—*Mastery*

z. Know the techniques for re-teaching and the motivational problems associated with re-teaching—*Mastery*

aa. Incorporate assessment and re-teaching into practices and competitions—*Application*

Model Competencies
Level 5

Domain: Injuries: Prevention, Care and Management

Standard 6. Demonstrate skill in the prevention, recognition and evaluation of injuries and the ability to assist athletes with the recovery/rehabilitation from injuries that are generally associated with participation in athletics in accordance with guidelines provided by qualified medical personnel.

Management

n.   Teach athletes that rehabilitation of injuries should be initiated under the guidance of medical personnel—*Mastery*

p.   Help athletes realize how such issues as "playing with pain" influence decisions about recovery programs and the time allotted to them—*Mastery*

r.   Emphasize to athletes that such elements as communication with care givers and skills for coping with becoming dependent upon medical personnel are part of the recovery program—*Mastery*

Domain: Growth, Development and Learning

Standard 13. Recognize the developmental physical changes that occur as athletes move from youth through adulthood and know how these changes influence the sequential learning and performance of motor skills in a specific sport.

a.   Demonstrate knowledge of the general developmental sequence in mental, motor and physical abilities—*Mastery*

Standard 15. Analyze human performance in terms of developmental information and individual body structure.

e.   Recognize differences in body structures specific to the age group and sport being coached—*Mastery*

f.   Know the basic movement capabilities and limitations of various body parts—*Mastery*

g.   Know the limitations on physical performance of the various elements involved in the body movement—*Mastery*

h.   Understand the essentials of anatomy and biomechanics as they relate to physical activity generally and specifically—*Mastery*

i.   Understand how biomechanical factors can limit motor performance skills—*Mastery*

    j.   Establish performance goals that reflect the developmental levels of the athletes—*Mastery*

    k.   Know how the body type of athletes affects their performance of the needed motor skills—*Mastery*

    l.   Know the athlete may extend the limits of their abilities by learning to compensate for specific limitations—*Mastery*

Domain: Training, Conditioning and Nutrition

Standard 18. Demonstrate a basic knowledge of physiological systems and their responses to training and conditioning.

    g.   Considering the sport being coached and individual differences of athletes, apply the principles of conditioning to the needs of athletes—*Mastery*

Standard 19. Design programs of training and conditioning that properly incorporate the mechanics of movement and sound physiological principles taking into consideration each individual's ability and medical history, avoiding contraindicated exercises and activities and guarding against the possibility of over-training; be able to modify programs as needed.

    d.   Assess the existing sport-specific fitness levelsof the athletes—*Mastery*

    k.   Know the indicators of over-training (i.e. lack of interest in practice, lowered levels of performance, minor injuries failing to heal or chronic complaining about practice or injury); regularly assess the athletes coached for these indicators—*Mastery*

    l.   Know techniques to mediate/reduce

over-training (i.e. increased variety of drills/activities allowing athletes to organize practices, shortening practice sessions and practicing at different times or in different settings) to reduce or eliminate these symptoms—*Mastery*

    m.   Know how to prevent over-training; these may include such things as cross-training, periodization and increased autonomy—*Mastery*

Domain: Social/psychological Aspects of Coaching

Standard 23. Identify and interpret to co-coaches, athletes, concerned others and the general public the values that are to be developed from participation in sports programs.

    g.   Relate to athletes instances in which ethical conduct translates from sport to life in general—*Mastery*

    h.   Prepare athletes to deal with media representatives; teach athletes how to interact with persons representing the media in discussions of such issues as evaluation of competition and career objectives—*Mastery*

Standard 24. Identify and apply ethical conduct in sport by maintaining emotional control and demonstrating respect for athletes, officials and other coaches.

f. Learn stress management techniques such as progressive relaxation, deep breathing, behavior modeling, visualization and positive self-talk and be able to teach them to the athletes; assist athletes in using these techniques to deal with competitive stress— *Mastery*

g. Use stress management skills to defuse potentially difficult emotional situations—*Mastery*

Standard 27. Be sufficiently familiar with the basic principles of goal setting to motivate athletes toward immediate and long range goals.

d. Assist athletes in relating long-range goals for participation to the realities of competition and the need to develop non-sports related interests and talents on the part of everyone involved—*Mastery*

Standard 28. Treat each athlete as an individual while recognizing the dynamic relationship of personality and socio-cultural variables such as gender, race and socio-economic differences.

a. Recognize that social environment influences the behaviors and personalities of athletes—*Mastery*

b. Understand how social, cultural and emotional forces interact in creating athlete personalities—*Mastery*

c. Understand the many dimensions of personality that may be expressed in athletics and teach athletes how to deal with these differences—*Mastery*

d. Accept differences in personality as another necessary component in preparing athletes for competition—*Mastery*

Domain: Skills, Tactics and Strategies

Standard 30. Identify and apply specific competitive tactics and strategies appropriate for the age and skill levels involved.

j. Understand how rules may dictate strategy, and be able to implement appropriate strategies in competitive situations—*Mastery*

Standard 31. Organize and implement materials for scouting, planning practices and analysis of games.

h. Be able to anticipate the likely strategies of opposing coaches and be prepared to respond to them in a timely manner—*Mastery*

i. Be able to identify the basic philosophy guiding the play of opponents—*Mastery*

j.   Use knowledge of the opponent strategies, tactics and philosophy to aid in the preparation of game plans and the selection of strategies and tactics—*Mastery*

Standard 33. Organize, conduct and evaluate practice sessions with regard to established program goals that are appropriate for different stages of the season.

c.   Teach the skills and tactics through practice activities that reflect competitive experiences—*Mastery*

d.   Stress performance as the measure of progress in learning skills—*Mastery*

f.   Use season analysis and summary along with the seasonal and individual practice schedules to assist in planning for the succeeding season—*Mastery*

g.   Evaluate the progress of individual athletes in achieving pre-determined goals—*Mastery*

h.   Consult with experienced coaches and educators for aid in assessing the athlete progress—*Mastery*

Domain: Teaching and Administration

Standard 34. Know the key elements of sport principles and technical skills as well as the various teaching methods that can be used to introduce and refine them.

c.   Know and apply steps for systematically instructing athletes as they progress developmentally in the skills of the sport—*Mastery*

i.   Determine when it is necessary to re-instruct athletes in such elements as skills, strategies and rules—*Mastery*

j.   Know and use the most effective instructional techniques of re-teaching—*Mastery*

k.   Know and use different motivational techniques and reward systems in preparing athletes for sessions involving re-instruction and review—*Mastery*

l.   Use appropriate tools such as videotapes to analyze skills and to monitor skills in both practice and competition settings—*Mastery*

m.   Use assessment during practice to guide instruction and re-instruction—*Mastery*

Standard 35. Demonstrate objective and effective procedures for the evaluation and selection of personnel involved in the athletic program and for periodic program reviews.

j.   Prepare a list of performance objectives for additional personnel—*Mastery*

l.   Use formal, written evaluations to assist in selecting and retaining program personnel—*Mastery*

Domain: Professional Preparation and Development

Standard 37. Acquire sufficient practical field experience and supervision in the essential coaching areas to ensure an adequate level of coaching competence for the level of sport coached. This would include a variety of knowledge, skills and experiences. The coach should:

a. Know the appropriate sequence used to teach necessary skills to developing athletes and the means for assessing the skill level and progress of athletes—*Mastery*

b. Prepare a season plan considering the abilities of in-coming athletes and maximum facilitation of their skills during the season—*Mastery*

c. Prepare practice plans that reflect reasonable time allowances for skill development in consideration of the sequential nature of skill acquisition—*Mastery*

d. Prepare written practice plans that follow guidelines for effective instruction and meeting the athlete needs—*Mastery*

e. Evaluate athletes during practice sessions; identify those who are able to enter higher levels of competition on the basis of predetermined criteria, such as skill, ability, adherence to rules and social/psychological considerations—*Mastery*

f. Assign positions, events and develop line-ups, orders and rotations that reflect the capabilities and readiness of the athletes—*Mastery*

g. Select skills and strategies appropriate to the sport and choose those that are consistent with athlete abilities—*Mastery*

h. Make appropriate coaching decisions during competition and adjust decisions based on situation—such as changes in strategy or tactics, safety considerations or competitive flow—*Mastery*

i. Teach the rules governing competition to all athletes—*Mastery*

j. Evaluate team play and individual performance in order to correct errors and facilitate maximum performance—*Mastery*

k. Evaluate player development and team play over the course of a season—*Mastery*

l. Deal effectively and sensitively with parents and guardians and/or others concerned with individual athletes—*Mastery*

m. Relate positively to officials, opposing coaches and athletes, and spectators—*Mastery*

n. Be aware of current developments in the sport through attending clinics and workshops, reading professional publications and communicating with other coaches and professionals—*Mastery*

o. Utilize guidelines for effective instruction—*Mastery*

p. Emphasize and foster self-control and self-discipline by athletes—*Mastery*

q. Evaluate effectiveness of drills—*Mastery*

r. Prepare desired outcomes for the athletic program which emphasize the growth and development of athletes—*Mastery*

s. Sequence practices so that athletes become increasingly responsible for themselves and elements of practice—*Mastery*

t. Demonstrate the ability to communicate effectively using audio-visual resources—*Mastery*

v. At regular intervals, seek feedback from experienced coaches or assistants to evaluate practice sessions; discuss their observations and implement changes—*Mastery*

x. Apply scientific and experiential information to the improvement of the specific sport—*Mastery*

aa. Incorporate assessment and re-teaching into practices and competitions—*Mastery*

National Standards for Athletic Coaches

A Summary of Competencies by Domain and Coaching Level

Interpreting the Matrix

The following three pages form a matrix which summarizes the previous information by level and domain. Across the top are listed the eight domains covered in the Standards and down the left margin are the five levels of preparation. The 40 cells in this table provide a guide for using the Standards and for coaching education. The last column of the table shows the total number of competencies dealt with at each level.

The competencies in the text are defined for the coach in practical application. Using the terms *Awareness, Application* and *Mastery,* the degree of knowledge of each competency that the individual coach has achieved can be identified. After a competency has been mastered it now becomes internalized, this is not written specifically in the competencies, but is expected throughout.

In contrast, this matrix is defined in terms of coaching education and what levels of learning should be taking place in a classroom setting, thus the use of *Introduction, Review, Master* and *Refine.* The letters in parenthesis reflect the recommended treatment of this concept or skill in the coaching education context. "I" refers to *Introduction,* "Rv" refers to *Review,* "M" refers to *Mastered,* and "Rf" refers to *Refine.* The absence of a parenthetical notation following the lower case letters indicates that the competency will be learned by the student at that particular level.

The easiest way to develop an understanding of the matrix table is to consider some examples drawn from it.

In the matrix under **Injuries: Prevention, Care and Management** at Level 1 are presented such items as 1a and 4f(I). This means that point 1a will be learned by all coaches as they consider their Level 1 materials. Similarly, objective 4f is covered, but the parenthetical notation "I" indicates that this subject is only *Introduced.* At the initial level of study, such topics will be presented and briefly discussed; however, they will be treated in more detail at later levels of coaching education. For instance, Level 2 coaches would be introduced to the idea that clothing worn for practices and competitions may increase the risk to athletes (4d). Elsewhere in the table, the notations "Rv," "M" and "Rf" appear. "Rv" and "Rf" initially seem similar, but there are differences. "Rv" refers to a topic being *Reviewed.* This means that coaches should be involved in a follow-up discussion of factual information or actions to be taken, such as the need to contact medical personnel in the case of other than minor injury (7g). "Rf" indicates that elements of the competency will be *Refined.* This refers to skills or attitudes that will require further study. For example, this applies to the ability to recognize how athletes vary in their ability to deal with circulatory stress (4b). "M" shows that a competency is to be *Mastered* at a particular level. Thus, at Level 4 coaches will be fully able to instruct athletes in the need to have injury rehabilitation programs guided by medical personnel (6q). As noted, once a topic has been learned, it will remain a part of the coaches' repertoire to be used in later study.

Level	Injuries: Prevention, Care and Management	Risk Management	Growth, Development and Learning
1	1a, 1b, 1c, 1d, 1e, 1f, 2a, 2b, 3b, 4f(I), 4g(I), 5a, 5b(I), 5c, 5d, 6a, 6d, 6e, 6f, 6g, 6h, 6i, 6j, 6q, 7f(I) (n = 25)	9a, 9b, 9c 9d, 9e, 9f, 9g(I), 10a, 10b, 10c(I), 10d(I), 11b, 11c, 12a, 12e (n = 15)	13b(I), 13c(I), 13d(I), 14b(I), 14c(I), 15b, 15c(I), 16b(I), 16d(I), 17a(I), 17b(I) (n = 11)
2	1g(I), 2c, 2d,3f, 4b(I), 4c(I), 4d(I), 4e(I), 4f(Rv), 4g(Rv), 5b(M), 6a, 6b, 6e, 6f, 6g, 6h, 6i, 6j, 6l, 6q, 7a, 7b, 7f(Rv), 7g, 8b(I), 8c(I) (n = 26)	9a, 9b, 9c 9d, 9e, 9f, 9g(Rv), 9h, 10a, 10b, 10c(M), 10d(M), 11a, 11b, 11c, 12a, 12e (n = 17)	13a(I), 13b(Rf), 13c(Rf), 13d(Rf), 14a(I), 14b(Rv), 14c(Rv), 14f(I), 15a, 15c(M), 15d(I), 16b(Rv), 16d(Rv), 17a(Rf), 17b(Rf), 17c(I) (n = 16)
3	1g(M), 3a, 3c, 3d, 3e, 3g, 3h, 3i, 4a, 4b(Rf), 4c(Rf), 4d(Rf), 4e(Rf), 4f(Rv), 4g(Rv), 6a, 6c(I), 6d, 6e, 6f, 6g, 6h, 6i, 6j, 6l, 6k(I), 6l(I), 6q(I), (I), 6o(I), 6p(I), 6q, 6r(I), 7c(I), 7d, 7e, 7f(Rv), 8a, 8b(M), 8c(M) (n =39)	9a, 9b, 9c 9d, 9e, 9f, 9g(Rv), (M), 10a, 10b, 11a, 11b, 11c, 12a, 12b, 12c, 12d, 12e (n = 17)	13a(Rv), 13b(M), 13c(M), 13d(M), 13e(I), 14a(Rf), 14b(Rv), 14c(Rv), 14d(I), 14e(I), 14f(Rv), 15d(M), 15e(I), 15f(I), 15g(I), 15h(I), (I), 15i(I), (I), 15j(I), 15k(I), 15l(I), 15m, 15n, 15o(I), 15r(I), (I), 16a(I), 16b(Rv), 16c(I), 16d(Rv), 16e(I), 16f(I), 16g(I), 1(I), 17a(M), 17b(M), 17c(Rf) (n = 34)
4	1h, 3j, 4b(Rf), 4e(Rf), 4f(Rv), 4g(Rv), 6a, 6c(Rf), 6d, 6e, 6f, 6g, 6h, 6i, 6j, 6l, 6k(Rf), 6l(Rf), 6q(Rf), (Rf), 6o(Rf), 6p(Rf), 6l, 6r(Rf), 7c(M), 7f(Rv), 8d (n = 26)	9a, 9b, 9c, 9d, 9e, 9f, 10a, 10b, 11a, 11b, 11c, 12a, 12b, 12c, 12d, 12e (n = 16)	13a(M), 13e(M), 14a(Rf), 14b(Rv), 14c(Rv), 14d(Rv), 14e(Rf),14f(Rf), 15e(M), 15f(Rf), 15g(M), 15h(M), (Rf), 15i(Rf), (Rf), 15j(Rf), 15k(Rf), 15l(Rf), 15o(Rf), 15r(M), (M), 16a(Rv), 16b(Rv), 16c(Rv), 16d(Rv), 16e(Rf), 16f(Rf), 16g(Rf), 1(Rf), 17c(M) (n =26)
5	1h, 4b(Rf), 4e(Rf), 4f(Rv), 4g(Rv), 6a, 6d, 6e, 6f, 6g, 6j, 6l, (M), 6p(M), 6q, 6r(M), 7f(Rv) (n = 22)	9a, 9b, 9c, 9d, 9e, 9f, 10a, 10b, 11a, 11b, 11c, 12a, 12b, 12c, 12d, 12e (n = 16)	13a(M), 14a(Rf), 14b(Rv), 14c(Rv), 14d(Rv), 14e(Rf), 15e(M), 15f(M), 15g(M), 15h(M), (M), (M), 15j(M), 15l(M), 16a(Rv), 16b(Rv), 16c(Rv), 16d(Rv), 16e(Rf), 16f(Rf), 16g(Rf), 1(Rf) (n = 24)

Level	Training, Conditioning and Nutrition	Social/ Psychological Aspects	Skills, Tactics and Strategies
1	19a(I), 19b(I), 19c(I), 21c(I) (n = 4)	22a(I), 22b(I), 22c(I), 22d(I), 22e(I), 23a(I), 23b(I), 23c(I), 23d(I), 24a(I), 24b(I), 24c(I), 24d(I), 24e(I), 25a(I), 25b(I), 25c(I), 25d(I), 26a(I), 26b(I), 26c(I), 26f(I), 29a(I), 29b(I) (n = 24)	30a(I), 30b(I), 30c(I), 30d(I), 30f(I), 31a(I), 32a(I), 32b(I), 32c(I), 33a(I), 33b(I), 33e(I) (n = 12)
2	18a(I), 19a(M), 19b(M), 19c(Rv), 20b(I), 21b(I), 21c(Rv), (I) (n = 8)	22a(Rv), 22b(Rv), 22c(Rv), 22d(Rv), 22e(Rv), 22f(I), 22g(I), 22h(I), 23a(Rv), 23b(Rv), 23c(Rv), 23d(Rv), 23e(I), 24a(Rf), 24b(Rf), 24c(Rf), 24d(Rf), 24e(Rf), 25a(M), 25b(M), 25c(M), 25d(Rv), 26a(Rv), 26b(Rv), 26c(Rv), 26d(I), 26e(I), 26f(Rf), 27a(I), 27c(I), 29a(Rf), 29b(Rf), 29c(I), 29d(I) (n=34)	30a(Rf), 30b(Rf), 30c(Rf), 30d(Rf), 30e(I), 30f(Rf), 30g(I), 31a(Rv), 31b(I), 32a(Rv), 32b(Rv), 32c(Rv), 32d(I), 33a(Rf), 33b(Rf), 33e(Rf) (n = 16)
3	18a(M), 18b, 18c, 18d, 18e(I), 18f(I), 18g(I), 19c(M), 19d(I), 19e(I), 19f(I), 19g(I), 19h(I), (I), 19i(I), 19j(I), 19k(I), (I), 19l(I), 20a(I), 20b(Rv), 20c(I), 20d(I), 20e(I), 20f(I), 20g(I), 21a(I), 21b(Rv), 21c(Rv), (Rf), 21d(I), 21e(I), 21f(I), 21g(I), 21h(I) (n = 32)	22a(Rv), 22b(Rv), 22c(Rv), 22d(Rv), 22e(Rv), 22f(Rv), 22g(Rv), 22h(Rv), 22i(I), 22j(I), 23a(Rv), 23b(Rv), 23c(Rv), 23d(Rv), 23e(Rf), 23f(I), 23g(I), , 24a(Rf), 24b(Rf), 24c(Rf), 24d(Rf), 24e(Rf), 24f(I), 24g(I), 25d(Rv), 25e(I), 26a(Rv), 26b(Rv), 26c(Rv), 26d(Rf), 26e(Rf), 26f(Rf), 27a(Rf), 27b(I), 27c(Rf), 27d(I), 28a(I), 28b(I), 28c(I), 28d(I), 29a(Rf), 29b(Rf), 29c(Rf), 29d(Rf), 29e(I) (n = 45)	30a(Rf), 30b(Rf), 30c(M), 30d(M), 30e(Rf), 30f(M), 30g(Rv), 30h(I), 30i(I), 30j(I), 31a(M), 31b(M), 31c(I), 31d(I), 31e(I), 31f(I), 31g(I), 31h(I), 32a(Rv), 32b(Rv), 32c(Rv), 32d(Rv), 33a(M), 33b(M), 33c(I), 33d(I), 33e(Rf), 33f(I), 33g(I), 33h(I) (n = 30)
4	18e(M), 18f(M), 18g(Rf), 19d(Rf), 19e(M), 19f(M), 19g(M), 19h(M), (M), 19i(M), 19j(M), 19k(Rf), (Rf), 19l(Rf), 19m(I), 20a(Rv), 20b(Rv), 20c(Rv), 20d(Rv), 20e(Rv), 20f(Rf), 20g(Rf), 21a(Rv), 21b(Rv), 21c(Rv), (Rf), 21d(Rf), 21e(Rf), 21f(Rf), 21g(Rv), 21h(Rf) (n = 28)	22a(Rv), 22b(Rv), 22c(Rv), 22d(Rv), 22e(Rv), 22f(Rv), 22g(Rv), 22h(Rv), 22i(Rf), 22j(Rf), 23a(Rv), 23b(Rv), 23c(Rv), 23d(Rv), 23e(Rf), 23f(Rf), 23g(Rf), , 21h(I), 24a(Rf), 24b(Rf), 24c(Rf), 24d(Rf), 24e(Rf), 24f(Rf), 24g(Rf), 25d(Rv), 25e(M), 26a(Rv), 26b(Rv), 26c(Rv), 26d(Rf), 26e(Rf), 26f(Rf), 27a(Rf), 27b(Rf), 27c(Rf), 27d(Rf), 28a(Rf), 28b(Rf), 28c(Rf), 28d(Rf), 28e, 29a(Rf), 29b(Rf), 29c(Rf), 29d(Rf), 29e(Rf) (n = 48)	30a(Rf), 30b(Rf), 30e(M), 30g(Rv), 30h(Rf), 30i(Rf), 30j(Rf), 31c(M), 31d(M), 31e(M), 31f(M), 31g(M), 31h(Rv), 31i(I), 31j(I), 32a(Rv), 32b(Rv), 32c(Rv), 3d(Rv), 33c(Rf), 33d(Rf), 33f(Rf), 33g(Rf), 33h(Rf) (n = 24)
5	18g(M), 19d(M), 19k(M), (M), 19l(M), 19m(M), 20a(Rv), 20b(Rv), 20c(Rv), 20d(Rv), 20e(Rv), 20f(Rf), 20g(Rv), 21a(Rv), 21b(Rv), 21c(Rv), (Rf), 21d(Rf), 21e(Rf), 21f(Rf), 21g(Rf), 21h(Rf) (n = 20)	22a(Rv), 22b(Rv), 22c(Rv), 22d(Rv), 22e(Rv), 22f(Rv), 22g(Rv), 22h(Rv), 22i(Rf), 22j(Rv), 23a(Rv), 23b(Rv), 23c(Rv), 23d(Rv), 23e(Rf), 23f(Rf), 23g(Rf), , 21h(Rv), 24a(Rf), 24b(Rf), 24c(Rf), 24d(Rf), 24e(Rf), 24f(M), 24g(M), 25d(Rv), 26a(Rv), 26b(Rv), 26c(Rv), 26d(Rf), 26e(Rf), 26f(Rf), 27a(Rf), 27b(Rf), 27c(Rf), 27d(Rf), 28a(M), 28b(M), 28c(M), 28d(M), 28e, 29a(Rf), 29b(Rf), 29c(Rf), 29d(Rf), 29e(Rf) (n = 46)	30a(Rf), 30b(Rf), 30g(Rv), 30h(Rf), 30i(Rf), 30j(Rf), 31h(M), 31i(Rf), 31j(Rf), 32a(Rv), 32b(Rv), 32c(Rv), 32d(Rv), 33c(M), 33d(M), 33f(M), 33g(M), 33h(M) (n = 18)

Level	Teaching and Administration	Professional Preparation and Development	Total Competencies
1	34a(I), 34b(I), 34c(I), 34d(I) (n = 4)	36a(I), 36b(I), 36c(I), 36d(I) (n = 4)	**99**
2	34a(Rv), 34b(Rv), 34c(Rf), 34d(Rf), 34e(I), 35a(I), 35b(I), 35c(I), 35d(I), 35e(I) (n = 10)	36a(M), 36b(M), 36c(M), 36d(M), 36g(I), 36h(I), 37a(I), 37b(I), 37c(I), 37d(I), 37e(I), 37f(I), 37g(I), 37h(I), 37i(I), 37j(I), 37k(I), 37l(I), 37m(I), 37n(I), (I), 37p(I), 37q(I), 37r(I), 37s(I), 37t(I), 37v (n = 26)	**153**
3	34a(M), 34b(Rv), 34c(Rf), 34d(M), 34e(M), 34f(I), 34g, 34h, 35a(M), 35b(M), 35c(M), 35d(M), 35e(M), 35f(I), 35g(I), 35h(I), 35i(I), 35j(I), 35k(I), 35l(I), 35m(I) (n = 20)	36a, 36e(M), 36f(M), 36g(M), 36h(Rf), 36i(I), 37a(Rf), 37b(Rf), 37c(Rf), 37d(Rf), 37e(Rf), 37f(Rf), 37g(Rf), 37h(Rf), 37i(Rf), 37j(Rf), 37k(Rf), 37l(Rf), 37m(Rf), 37n(Rf), ,37p(Rf), 37q(Rf), 37r(Rf), 37s(Rf), 37t(Rf), 37u(I), 37v, 37w, 37x, 37y(I), 37z, 37bb, 37cc, (n = 33)	**250**
4	34b(Rv), 34c(M), 34f(M), 34i(I), 34j(I), 34k(I), 34l(I), 34m(I), 35f(M), 35g(M), 35h(Rf), 35i(Rf), 35j(Rf), 35k(Rf), 35l(Rf), 35m(Rf) (n = 16)	36e(M), 36f(M), 36h(M), 36i(Rf), 37a(Rf), 37b(Rf), 37c(Rf), 37d(Rf), 37e(Rf), 37f(Rf), 37g(Rf), 37h(Rf), 37i(Rf), 37j(Rf), 37k(Rf), 37l(Rf), 37m(Rf), 37n(Rf), 37p(Rf), 37q(Rf), 37r(Rf), 37s(Rf), 37t(Rf), 37u(Rf), 37v, 37w, 37x, 37y(Rf), 37z, 37bb, 37cc, (n = 32)	**247**
5	34b(Rv), 34c(M), 34i(Rf), 34j(Rf), 34k(Rf), 34l(Rf), 34m(Rf), 35h(Rf), 35i(Rf), 35j(Rf), 35k(Rf), 35l(Rf), 35m(Rf) (n = 13)	36i(Rf), 37a(M), 37b(M), 37c(M), 37d(M), 37e(M), 37f(M), 37g(M), 37h(M), 37i(M), 37j(M), 37k(M), 37l(M), 37m(M), 37n(M), (M), 37p(M), 37q(M), 37r(M), 37s(M), 37t(M), 37u(M), 37v, 37w, 37x, 37y(M), 37z, , 37bb, 37cc, (n = 27)	**208**

Glossary

Glossary

aerobic—Endurance activities and conditioning for them. These involve long-duration, low-intensity exercise and energy production using oxygen.

anaerobic—High-speed activities and conditioning for them. These involve sprint-type exercise and an energy production system that releases energy quickly while not using oxygen in the process. This relatively inefficient system produces large quantities of lactic acid in the muscles and can be supported for only relatively short periods of time.

BBPs—Blood-born pathogens. This term describes a number of diseases that spread primarily through contact with blood and other bodily fluids. Of greatest concern currently are hepatitis-B and HIV (human immuno-deficiency virus).

biomechanical—Describes the athletes' functioning in terms of mechanical principles. This includes such concepts as the generation and dissipation of forces, joints being hinges and extremities being levers.

chemical health—Describes the complex set of behaviors and attitudes focused on the athletes' relationship with such agents as drugs, alcohol and tobacco products. As with any element of health, athletes may exhibit healthy or unhealthy characteristics.

circuit training—A regimen involving participation in a variety of activities in rapid succession.

competencies—The specific knowledge, skills and values that coaches must know and do. Among the approximately 320 statements are ones such as, "Stop or modify practice or play when unsafe conditions exist" and "Know applicable safety standards for the sport coaches; regularly inspect equipment for conformance." Whether coaches have these competencies should be revealed in their behavior—how they act, what they do.

contraindicated—Potentially harmful or inadvisable. This term describes training, conditioning and stretching activities which either increase the risk of injury to an athlete or may actually represent a risk to athletes. Examples might include the traditional hurdler's stretch, repeated squatting or excessive jumping.

CPR—Cardio-pulmonary resuscitation. CPR specifically refers to a formal training program providing instruction in dealing with medical emergencies in which breathing or heart function is impaired.

domains—For these standards, the eight general areas of knowledge and experience necessary for success in coaching. They include: *Injuries:*

Prevention, Care and Recovery; *Risk Management*; *Growth, Development and Learning*; *Training, Conditioning and Nutrition*; *Social/psychological Aspects of Coaching*; *Skills, Tactics and Strategies*; *Teaching and Administration* and *Professional Preparation and Development*

effective instruction—Instruction in skills, rules, tactics and strategies that follows a series of generally accepted principles of teaching. Commonly recognized guidelines include these: set realistic expectations for the athletes, plan the instruction, create an orderly environment, group athletes by ability, maximize on-task time, maximize success, monitor the athletes' progress, ask questions about performance and learning and allow the athletes a sense of self-control.

first aid—Formal preparation in dealing with medical emergencies. This may be a sport-specific program or one offered by an agency such as the American Red Cross.

interval training—A regimen that alternates periods of vigorous exercise with recovery periods. Both aerobic and anaerobic activities and conditioning are involved.

level—As applied to these standards, one of the five steps within the proposed program. Beginning with level one and proceeding through level five, these levels generally correspond to increasing experience, involvement and responsibility of the coach, growing commitment to coaching as a profession, heightened competitiveness of play and working with more experienced athletes.

medical personnel or **medical professionals**—Any of the various people who traditionally work with injured athletes. These individuals are prepared for dealing with injuries by their training and experience. These groups may include—but not be limited to—NATA certified athletic trainers, emergency medical technicians, medical and osteopathic physicians, surgeons, chiropractors, dentists and rehabilitation therapists.

motor (performance) skills—Physical skills involving the entire body. These require athletes to use their coordination, balance, agility, power, strength and endurance.

overload—Applying a stress to the muscular systems. This involves a training program that requires the athletes to work harder than they normally do. This can be accomplished by increasing the load placed on the athletes, by having them do more repetitions of the activity, by having the activity continue for a longer time or by increasing the frequency of activity.

over-training—The idea that athletes may spend too much time and energy preparing for their sport. This condition is most often revealed in its effects: staleness, a lack of interest in practice, decreased levels of performance, increased injury rates related to "overuse."

pharmacological aids—Chemicals or medical procedures used with the idea of enhancing athletic performance. Steroids, amphetamines, caffeine, various tranquilizers, and numerous other drugs have been used in this manner. "Blood doping" also is included in this category of aids.

progression—A principle of conditioning which acknowledges the need to begin activity at a level the athletes can accommodate and to progress gradually to an increased work level.

reversibility—The loss of conditioning. During the competitive season athletes may actually lose some of the conditioning gains made during the off-season or in pre-season training. A maintenance program should be developed for all participants.

R.I.C.E.—Rest, Ice, Compression, Elevation. Many common athletic injuries can be treated with the R.I.C.E. formula, which involves resting the injured element, placing ice on the injury, compressing the injured area with some sort of dressing and elevating the injury above the level of the chest.

specificity—Describes the relationship between the training program and its outcomes. Each exercise, each activity produces certain results. These must be assessed in terms of a particular sport's requirements and the ability of the treatment, drill or tactic to bring about the desired outcome.

standards of care—These thirty-seven statements generally describing the actions and accountabilities of coaches. These standards outline various areas in which coaches have responsibility. For example coaches must "Prevent injuries by recognizing and insisting on safe playing conditions" and "Identify and apply specific competitive tactics and strategies appropriate for the age and skill levels involved."

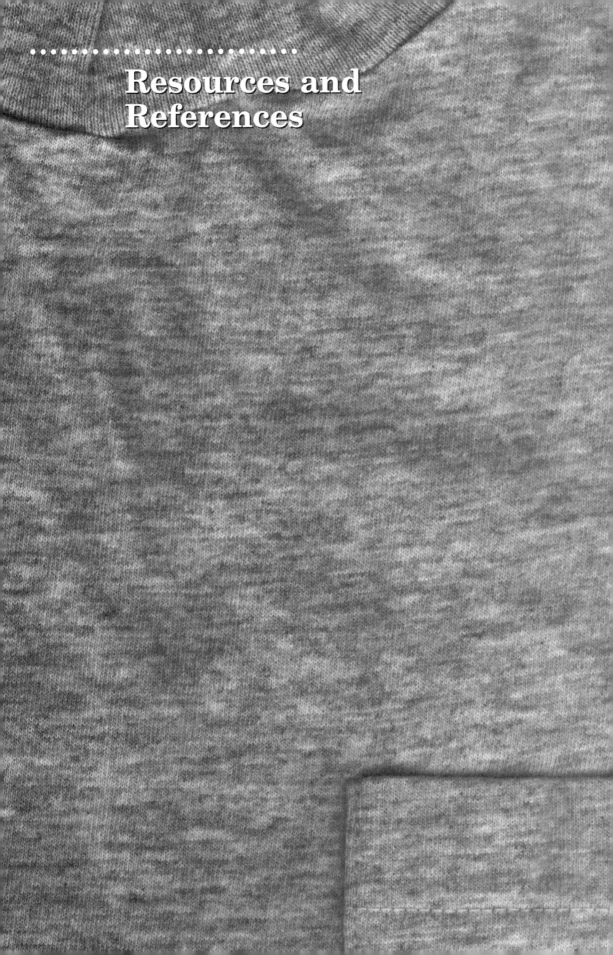

Resources and References

Resources

American Red Cross. (1991). *First aid: Responding to emergencies.* Mosby Year Book.

American Red Cross. (1991). *Standard first aid.* Author.

Canadian National Certification Program. (1989). *The course conductor: Levels 1-5, theory.* Gloucester, Ontario: The Coaching Association of Canada.

Coalition of Americans to Protect Sports (CAPS). (1994). Injury risk management and the keys. In *Sports.* North Palm Beach, FL: Author.

Eylenbosch, W. & Noah, N. (1988). *Surveillance in health and disease.* New York: Oxford University Press.

Flegel, M. (1992). *Sports first aid.* Champaign, IL: Human Kinetics.

Institute for the Study of Youth Sports. (1993). *Program for Athletic Coaches Education.* Dubuque, IA: Brown and Benchmark.

Martens, R. (1990). *Successful coaching* (2nd ed.). Champaign, IL: Human Kinetics.

National High School Athletic Coaches' Association. (1991). *National coaches' certification program - study guide.* Maitland, FL: Author.

National Recreation and Parks Association. (1994). *Overview of local parks and recreation agency accreditation.* Author.

Middlestaldt, A. (1980). *The volunteer coaches training program.* Bohemia, NY.: New York State Sports Authority.

Midtlyng, J. (1991). *The aquatic council instruction and credentialing program handbook.* Reston, VA: The Aquatic Council/ The American Alliance for Health, Physical Education, Recreation and Dance.

Pike, F. (1980). *Towards better coaching.* Australian Coaching Council.

Public Health Sports. (1985). *Prevention of injuries* (Vol. 100, No. 6).

Sharkey, B. (1987). *The coaches guide to sport psychology.* Champaign, IL: Human Kinetics.

Summerfield, L. (1991). *Credentialing in the health, leisure, and movement professions.* Washington, DC.: American Association of Colleges for Teacher Education.

United States Cerebral Palsy Athletic Association. (1989). *Sport injury control manual.* Westland, MI: Author.

USA Hockey. (1991). *The coach's plan book.* Colorado Springs, CO: Author.

USA Hockey. (1993). *USA Hockey volunteer administrator's manual.* Colorado Springs, CO: Author.

YMCA. (1990). *Youth sports administrator's manual.* Champaign, IL: YMCA of the U.S.A., YMCA Program Store.

References Used in the Definition of Standards and Competencies

A

Adams, S. H. (1981). Training and using volunteer coaches. *Athletic Purchasing and Facilities, 11,* 10-14.

Adams, S. H. (1980). The athletic administrator's dilemna. *Athletic Purchasing and Facilities, 4,* 26-30.

Adams, S. H. (1980). Coaching certification based on competencies. *Interscholastic Athletic Administration, 6*(4), 19-20, 30.

Adams, S. H. (Ed.) (1979). Coaching certification: The time is now. *USSA News, 3*(4).

Adams, S. H. (1978, November). Certification in coaching: A Sorely needed aspect of education. *Athletic Purchasing and Facilities,* 20-22.

Aerobics and Fitness Association of America. (1993). *Education programs for fitness instructors and health professionals* [Brochure]. Sherman Oaks, CA: Author.

American Academy of Pediatrics (1987). Exercise for children who are mentally retarded. *The Physician and Sportsmedicine, 15*(12), 141-142.

American Academy of Pediatrics. (1983). Climatic heat stress and the exercising child. *The Physician and Sportsmedicine, 11*(8), 155, 159.

American Academy of Pediatrics. (1983). Weight training and weight lifting: Information for the pediatrician. *The Physician and Sports Medicine, 11*(3), 157-1161.

American Academy of Pediatrics Committee on Children with Handicaps. (1970, January). The asthmatic child and his participation in sports and physical education. *Pediatrics, 45*(1), 150-151.

American Academy of Pediatrics Committee on Pediatric Aspects of Physical Fitness and Sports. (1979, November). *Status report on the proposal for an educational seminar for coaches participating in extrascholastic competitive athletic events in the grade school age group.* San Antonio, TX: Author.

American Academy of Pediatrics Committee on Physical Fitness, Recreation, and Sports. (1981, May). *A national program for developing competency in youth sports coaching.* Evanston, IL: Author.

American Association for Health, Physical Education, and Recreation. (1973). *Evaluating the high school athletic program*. Washigton, DC: National Council of Secondary School Athletic Directors, Division of Men's Athletics.

American Association of Colleges for Teacher Education. (1986). Accreditation (Issue Brief No. 7). Washington, DC: Author.

American Association of Colleges for Teacher Education (1986). *Teacher certification 1983-1986*. East Lansing, MI: ERIC Clearinghouse on Teacher Education.

American Association of Colleges for Teacher Education. *Coaching certification*. Washington, DC: Author.

American Association of Colleges for Teacher Education. *National board for professional teaching standards*. Clearinghouse on Teacher Education. Washington, DC: Author.

American College of Sports Medicine. (1988, August). *Opinion statement on physical fitness in children and youth*. Indianapolis, IN: Author.

American College of Sports Medicine. (1988, August). *Position stands and opinion statements*. (Publication Version No. 9). Indianapolis, IN: Author.

American College of Sports Medicine. (1987). ASCM begins certifying aerobi instructors. *The Physician and Sportsmedicine, 15*(9), 58.

American College of Sports Medicine. (1984, July). Position stand on the use of anabolic-androgenic steriods in sports. *Sports Medicine Bulletin*.

American College of Sports Medicine. (1983). Position statement on proper and improper weight loss programs. *Medicine and Science In Sports and Exercise, 15*, IX-XIII.
American College of Sports Medicine. (1982). Position statement on the use of alcohol in sports. *Medicine and Science In Sports and Exercise, 14*, IX-XI.

American Medical Association. (1977, April). AMA statement - Weight loss in amateur wrestling. *Sports Medicine Bulletin, 12*, 11.

American Psychological Association. (1985). *Standards for educational and psychological testing*. Washington, DC: Author.

American Society for Testing and Materials. (1994, October). *ASTM mobile training module on accelerating standards development and publication*. Philadelphia, PA: ASTM.

American Sport Education Program. (1995, January). *Interscholastic coaching: From accidental occupation to profession*. Champaign, IL: Author.

American Swimming Coaches Association. (1985). *Education, certification, cooperation*. [Brochure].

Andrews, J. R. (1979). State licensure of athletic trainers. *The American Journal of Sports Medicine, 7*(4), 268.

Applied Exercise Science council of NASPE. (1993, June). *Basic standards for preparation for careers in exercise science*. Author.

Aquatic Council, American Alliance for Health, Physical Education, Recreation, and Dance. (1994). *Safety in high school physical education aquatic programs, A position paper of the aquatic council, AAHPERD*.

Association for the Advancement of Health Education. (1992). Certified health education specialist. *Journal of Health Education, 23*, 339-340.

Avery, C. S. (1991). Certification, What to know and where to go. *The Physician and Sportsmedicine, 19*(12), 133-137.

B

Ball, R. T. (1988). Coaching competence: A burning issue in athletics today. *National Coach, 23,* 39 & 42.

Barranco, S. D. (1978, November). Needed: A stand in favor of certified athletic trainers. *Virginia Medical Monthly, 105*(11), 811.

Barrett, W. O. (1991, October 16). Specialized accrediting: the debate goes on [Letter to the editor]. *The Chronicle of Higher Education,* p. B3.

Baumgarten, S. (1984). It can be done! A model youth sports program. *Journal of Physical Education, Recreation and Dance, 55,* 55-58.

Bazzano, C. (1991). When is a coach justified in bending the rules. *Strategies, 4,* 5-7.

Becker, B. (1986, March 19). Kids' coaches certification: Idea whose time has come. *The Grand Rapids Press.*

Berry, W. D. (1986, Spring). Considerations for hiring lifeguards. *The Maryland Journal of Health, Physical Education, Recreation, and Dance,* 15-16.

Bowlus, W. C. (1979). First priority: Certified trainers. *Journal of Physical Education and Recreation, 50,* 71-72.

Bowman, B. T. (1982). Recognition for quality in centers for young children. *Young Children, 37,* 33-34.

Brandt, R. (1985). Prerequisites to a more rewarding profession. *Educational Leadership, 43*(3), 5.

Bronzon, R. T. (1982). Preparing leaders for non-school youth sports. *Athletic Purchasing and Facilities, 6,* 12-16.

Brown, E. W. *Is coaching certification necessary*. East Lansing, MI: Institute for the Study of Youth Sports.

C

Campbell, S. (1993). Coaching education around the world. *Sport Science Review, 2*(2), 62-74.

Candel, M. (1979, June 17). Crash course for coaches. *Leisure Sports,* 1;4.

Carlson, D. (1979). Coaching positions related to fewer teaching positions. *Interscholastic Athletic Administration, 6*(1), 9-10, 15.

Carter, M. J. & Foret, C. (1987, September). The credentialing triad. *Alliance Update,* p. 5.

Certification battle: Marketing the NCCP hasn't been easy. (1985, March/April). *Coaching Review,* 26-27.

Certification board approved; Model plan OK'ed. (1981, November/December). *Dateline: NRPA, 4*(6), 2.

Chelladurai, P., & Saleh, S. D. (1978). Preferred leadership in sports. *Canadian Journal of Applied Sport Sciences, 3*(2), 85-92.

Christensen, C. & Boeh, D. (1978). *1978 coaching certification survey.* University of Illinois, Department of Physical Education.

Cinque, C. (1986). Aerobic instructor certification: Standards at last. *The Physician and Sportsmedicine, 14*(12), 171-177.

Coaches certification program moves forward. (1989). *National Coach, 25,* 16-18.

Coaching Association of Canada. (1993). *1993 Coaching Entrainement.* [Brochure]. Goucester, Ontario: Author.

Coaching Association of Canada. (1978, November). *Guide for the preparation of national technical coaching certification packages.* Ottawa, Ontario: Author.

Cohen, A. (1993). School daze. *Athletic Business, 17,* 24-27.

Colorado High School Activities Association. (1992). *Coaches manual procedures and regulations for coaching certification.* Aurora, CO: Author.

Committee on Atherosclerosis and Hypertension in Childhood of the Council on Cardiovascular Disease in the Young, American Heart Association. (1986). Coronary risk factor modification in children: Exercise. *Circulation, 14*(5), 1189A-1191A.

Corbitt, R. W., Cooper, D. L., Erickson, D. J., Kriss, F. C., Thornton, M. L., & Craig, T. T. (1975, January). Female athletics: A special communication from the committee on the medical aspects of sports of the American medical association. *Journal of Physical Education and Recreation.*

Council on Accreditation - National Recreation and Park Association. (1990, January). *Conceptual basis of revised curriculum standards.* Alexandria, VA: Author.

Council on Accreditation - National Recreation and Park Association. (1990, January). *Standards and evaluative criteria for recreation, park resources, and leisure services baccalaureate program.* Alexandria, VA: Author.

Council on Postsecondary Accreditation (COPA) (1994). *Standards for review.* Washington, D.C.: COPA.

Crawford, T. (1993, Fall). Where are we headed. *Olympic Coach, 3*(4), 1.

D

Dyment, P. G. (1988, May). New guidelines for sports participation. *The Physician and Sportsmedicine, 16*(5), 45-46.

E

Education and Work Program & Boise School District. (1990, October). *Boise school district athletic department program evaluation report and recommendations from Boise school district athletic advisory committee.* Boise, ID: Author.

Emery, E. M., McDermott, R. J., & Ritter, G. P. (1991). Toward a policy on regulation of the weight control industry. *Journal of Health Education, 22*(3), 150-153.

Esslinger, A. A. (1968, October). Certification for high school coaches. *JOHPER, 39,* 42-45.

Evans, V. (1977, October). What is a profession? *Physical Educator, 34*(3), 125-127.

Exer-Safety Association. (1993). *Why do smart instructors choose ESA's certification.* Orlando, FL: Author.

F

Fiegley, D. (1988). *1988 comparative analysis of youth sports educational programs prepared for the Rutgers youth sports research council.* Paper presented at the national conference of the American Alliance for Health Physical Education Recreation and Dance, Kansas City, MO.

Floden, R. E. (1978, February). *Analogy and credentialing* (Research Series No. 6). East Lansing, MI: Institute for Research on Teaching.

Foster, C. (1986). Certification: More than a personal commitment. *Sports Medicine Bulletin, 21,* 8.

Franklin, B. A. (1994). ASCM's certification: What it has meant to me. *Sports Medicine Bulletin, 29*(1), 5

Fredricks, D. (1985). The United States gymnastics safety association: Aleader in safety consciousness. *Journal of Physical Education, Recreation, and Dance, 56,* 45-46.

G

Geyelin, M. (1992, September 23). Injuries incurred by high-school athletes lead to more lawsuits against coaches. *The Wall Street Journal,* B1 & B7.

Gideonse, H. D. (1992, April 15). Accreditation standards in teacher education [Letter to the editor]. *The Chronicle of Higher Education,* p. B6.

Glossary of fitness, management and technical terms. (1991). *Fitness Management,* 193-209.

Goode, W. J. (1961). The librarian: From occupation to profession. *Library Quarterly, 31,* 306-318.

Gould, D. (1980, July) *Sport Psychology.* Paper presented at the U.S.W.F. National Wrestling Coaches Certification Program - Bronze Level, Iowa City, IA.

Gould, D., Giannini, J., Krane, V., & Hodge, K. (1988). *Educational needs of elite US national team, Pan American and olympic coaches.* Urbana-Champaign: University of Illinois, Department of Kinesiology.

Gowan, G. (1978). The final word. *Coaching Review, 1,* 60-62.

Grace, P. (1991). A report on the 1991 NATA board of certification examinations. *NATA News, 4*(3), 13-14.

Grace, P., & Ledderman, L. (1982). Role delineation study for the certification examination for entry-level athletic trainers. *Athletic Training, 17,* 264-265.

Graham, P. (1989). The other certification: More benefits than risks. *National Education Association Today, 7,* 75-79.

Grande, P. C. *Faculty and non-faculty coaches: A desriptive study.* Unpublished doctoral dissertation, University of Pennsylvania.

Gratto, J. (1983). Competencies used to evaluate high school coaches. *Journal of Physical Education, Recreation, and Dance, 54,* 59-60.

Greaney, L. (1994, May). Ensuring excellence without elitism [Letter to the editor]. *Fitness Management, 10,* 14-17.

Greninger, L. O. (1978). The Toledo experience: An accredited program in corrective therapy. *American Correctional Therapy Journal, 32*(1), 12-15.

Guide to national efforts to set subject-matter standards. (1993, June 16). *Education Week,* 17.

H

Haney, W. (1993, September 29). Preventing cheating on standardized tests. *The Chronicle of Higher Education,* B3.

Hart, B. A., Hasbrook, C. A. & Mathes, S. A. (1986). An examination of the reduction in the number of female interscholastic coaches. *Research Quarterly for Exercise and Sport, 57*(1), 68-77.

Harty, D. (1978, July 6). *National federation annual meeting.* Paper presented at the meeting of the National Federation Annual Meeting in Salt Lake City, UT.

Hawley, W. D. (Ed.). (1992). The alternative certification of teachers. *Teacher Education Monograph: No. 14.* Washington, DC: ERIC Clearinghous on Teacher Education.

Hayden, J. (1992, September/October). *Journal of Health Education, 23*(6), 341-346.

Hedley, B. (1991, April). Coach evaluation: an essential element in the learning process. *Dynamic Teaching, 1*(1), 1-2.

Heitmann, H. M. (1986). Teacher certification changes as a result of the Illinois education reform. *Illinois Journal of Health Physical Education & Recreation, 21,* 6.

Herbert, D. L. (1993). IRSA formally adopts new standards. *Fitness Management, 9,* 22-23.

Holmen, M. G., & Parkhouse, B. L. (1981). Trends in the selection of coaches for female athletes: A demographic inquiry. *Research Quarterly for Exercise and Sport, 52*(1), 9-18.

Houseworth, S. (1989, January). *Survey of Illinios high school athletic coaches and directors to determine areas of need for developing coaching education and certification.* Illinios State University.

I

Ideal solution to solving problems in major college sports. (1981, September). *The athletic educator's report, 857,* 1, 8.

Identifying performance standards. (1993, September). Paper presented at the USOC Coaching Symposium.

Indiana High School Athletic Association. (1980). *Handbook for Emergency Coaches in IHSAA Member Schools 1980-1981.* Indianapolis, IN: Author.

Institute for Athletics and Education. (1993, Summer). The IAH and national sport policy formation. *IAE Quarterly, 3*(2), 1.

Institute for Learning, a Divison of Institute for Management, Inc. (1977, March). *The Athletic Educator's Report* (Issue No. 805). Old Saybrook, CT: Author.

Institute for the Study of Youth Sports. (1988, November). *Certification of youth sports coaches: A proposal to the Athletic Council Michigan Recreation and Park Association.* East Lansing, MI: Author.

International Federation of Sports Medicine. (1991). Position statement: Excessive physical training in children and adolescents. *Clinical Journal of Sports Medicine, 1*(4), 262-264.

International Federation of Sports Medicine. (1990). Position statement: Physical exercise: An important factor for health. *The Physician and Sportsmedicine, 18*(3), 155-156.

J

Jackson, N. (1992). The five basic types of coaches found on today's pitch. *Soccer Journal, 37,* 36.

Jackson, V. D. (1984). Theoretical constructs underlying the process of content validation in health education research. *Health Education, 15,* 37-40.

Jaeger, R. M. (1992). *"World class" standards, choice, and privatization: Weak measurement serving presumptive policy.* Greensboro, NC: University of North Carolina at Greensboro.

Jaschik, S. (1994, May 4). A modest retreat on accrediting. *The Chronicle of Higher Education,* A31.

Jaschik, S. (1993, December 1). A threat to autonomy? *The Chronicle of Higher Education,* p. A25.

Johnson, J. L., Anderson, M.L. & Jonas, R. (1986). The Minnesota experience coaching certification. *JOPERD, 57,* 53-56.

Johnston, R. J. (1993). A reply: Standards aren't everything. *Athletic Business, 17,* 11.

Joint Committee of the Association for the Advancement of Health Education and the American School Health Association. (1992, September/October). *Journal of Health Education, 23*(6), 352-354.

Joint Committee on Physical Fitness, Recreation, and Sports Medicine. (1973, May). Athletic activities by children with skeletal abnormalities. *Pediatrics, 51*(5), 949-951.

Jones, A. A. (1995, January 6). Our stake in the history standards. *The Chronicle of Higher Education.* p. B1-B3.

Journal-based self-study for CHES recertification: A new service for AAHE members. (1992, September/October). *Journal of Health Education, 23*(6), 324-325.

K

Kauth, B. (1984). The athletic training major. *Journal of Health, Physical Education, Recreation, and Dance, 55,* 11-13.

Kelley, E. J., Brightwell, S. (1984, March). Should interscholastic coaches be certified. *Journal of Physical Education, Recreation, and Dance.*

Kemp, J. F. (1979, March 26). Extensions of remarks. *Congressional Record,* p. E1317.

Kennedy, M. M. (1989, Spring). Reflection and the problem of Profesional standards. *Colloquy, 2*(2), 1.

Kimiecik, J. C. (1988). Who needs coaches' education? US coaches do. *The Physician and Sportsmedicine, 16*(11), 124-136.

King, A. (1992, April 15). Accreditation standards in teacher education [Letter to the editor]. *The Chronicle of Higher Education,* p. B6.

Klieber, D. A. (1981). Searching for enjoyment in children's sports. *The Physical Educator, 38,* 77-84.

Koretz, D. (1989). The new National assessment: What it can and cannot do. *National Education Association Today, 7,* 32-37.

L

Lang, M. (1981, March). NAGWS surveys attitudes, seeks solutions. *Update.*

Leake, P. G. A. (1994, May). Ensuring excellence without elitism [Letter to the editor]. *Fitness Management, 10,* 14-17.

Leatherman, C. (1994, February 9). Accreditors fight back. *The Chronicle of Higher Education.* p. A21-A22.

Leatherman, C. (1993, January 6). Regional accrediting agencies face questions about why - and when - they sanction colleges. *The Chronicle of Higher Education,* p. A15.

Leatherman, C. (1991, September 18). Specialized accrediting agencies challenged by campus officials. *The Chronicle of Higher Education, 38*(4), A1.

LeCompte, D. (1989, May). Dance-exercise: Source of tomorrow's fitness leaders. *Fitness Management, 5,* 24-25.

Legwold, G. (1983). Injury rate lowered by high school trainers. *The Physician and Sportsmedicine, 11,* 35.

Legwold, G. (1983). Trainers seek regulation but find a catch 22. *The Physician and Sportsmedicine, 10*(11), 35.

Lewis, G. , & Appenzeller, H. (eds.) (1981). *Youth Sports: A Search for Direction.* Greensboro, NC:Sport Studies Foundation.

Lewis, R. S. (1993). Are athletic trainers necessary in high schools. *The First Aider, 64*(1), 1.

Lord, R. H., & Kozar, B. A test for volunteer youth sport coaches. *Journal of Sport Behavior, 5*(2), 77-82.

M

MacGregor, L. (1986). ABC's of a coaching creed. *Coaching Review, 9,* 39-42.

Maetozo, M. G. (Ed.). (1971). *Certification of high school coaches.* Washington, D.C.: American Association for Health Physical Education and Recreation.

Maetozo, M. G. (1971, April). Required specialized preparation for coaching. *Journal of Health, Physical Education and Recreation, 42*(4), 12-13.

Maetozo, M. G. (1981). Athletic coaching: Its future in a changing society. *JOPERD, 52,* 40-43.

Maetozo, M. G. (1981, March). NASPE active on "rent-a-coach" issue. *UPDATE.*

Maetozo, M. G. (1981, September). The future of athletic coaching. *The Education Digest, 47,* 38-41.

Maetozo, M. G. & Bosco, J. S. (1979). Certification and licensing of professionals in physical education and athletics. *Proceedings of NAPECS/NCPEAM National Conference* (pp. 247-255).

Maher, D. (1979, October). Coaching certification a necessity. *The Michigan Athletic Director, 1*(4).

Maron, B. J., & Mitchell, J. H. (1994). Revised eligibility recommendations for competitive athletes with cardiovascular abnormalities. *Medicine and Science in Sports and Exercise, 26*(10)

Martin, G. M., Gullickson, G., & Gerken, C. (1980, July). Graduate medical education and certification in physical medicine and rehabilitation. *Arch. Phys. Med. Rehabil., 61,* 291-297.

McCarthy, J. (1994, May). Ensuring excellence without elitism [Letter to the editor]. *Fitness Management, 10,* 14-17.

McKinney, W. C. & Taylor, R. (1970). Certification of coaches: The Missouri approach. *JOHPER, 41,* 50-56.

•••••••••••••••••••••••••••

Meinhardt, T. (1971). A rationale for certification of high school coaches in Illinois. *JOHPER, 42,* 48.

Metropolitan Park District of Tacoma, Washington. (1986). *Youth sport coaches association.* Tacoma, WA: Author.

Michigan Association for Health, Physical Education and Recreation's Board of Directors. (1980, May). *Statement of standards for athletic coaching.* Lansing, MI: Author.

Miller, D. (1981). Guidelines for the clarification of the role of developmental/adapted physical education and the therapies. *American Corrective Therapy Journal, 35*(3), 62-65.

Miller, H. S. (1980, April). The field of prevention and rehabilitation certification and licensing, what part does the ACSM play? *Sports Medicine Bulletin, 15*(2), 8.

Milne, C. (1990). Higher education for coaches - Preparation survey results. *Journal of Physical Education, Recreation, and Dance, 61,* 44-46.

Minnesota Board of Teaching. (1978, February). *Coaches of interscholastic sports in the elementary and secondary schools.*

Mitchell, J. H., Maron, B. J., & Raven, P. E. (Eds.). (1994). 26th Bethesda conference recommendations for determining eligibility for competition in athletes with cardiovascular abnormalities. *Medicine and Science in Sport and Exercise, 26*(Suppl. 10), S223-S283.

Montgomery, G. (1994, May). Ensuring excellence without elitism [Letter to the editor]. *Fitness Management, 10,* 14-17.

Mooney, C. J. (1992, May 6). Teacher-education programs debate the need for accrediting agency's stamp of approval. *The Chronicle of Higher Education,* A19.

MRPA/NRPA certification: Issues and answers. (1992, July). *Leisure Focus,* 6.

Mueller, F. O. & Robey, J. M. (1971). Factors related to the certification o high school footbal coaches. *JOHPER, 42,* 50-51.

Mundra, D. (1980, October). A humanist looks at coaching. *Journal of Physical Education and Recreation,* 22-25.

••

N

Nash, H. L. (1985). Instructor Certification: Making Fitness Programs Safer. *The Physician and Sportsmedicine, 13*(10), 142-155.

NATA board acts to protect members' certification from organized attack by competing organization. *NATA News, 4*(3), 9.

National Association for Girls and Women in Sport (1986). Position paper on coaching certification. *Colorado Journal of Health, Physical Education, Recreation, and Dance, 12,* 6-8.

National Association for Sport and Physical Education. (1992). Coaching children in sports. *NASPE News*. Issue No. 31. Kernersville, NC: Hutslar, J.

National Association for Sport and Physical Education. (1992, June). *NASPE Position statement on exploitation of the interscholastic athlete.*

National Association for Sport and Physical Education & North American Society for Sport Management. (1992). *General overview of the accreditation process.* Reston, VA: Author.

National Athletic Trainers Association Inc. *Careers placement.* [Brochure]. Greenville, NC: Author.

National Athletic Trainers Association. *The national athletic trainers association certification program.*

National Board for Professional Teaching Standards. (1993, April). *Draft report on standards for national board certification.* Washington, DC: Author.

National Board for Professional Teaching Standards. (1992). *Forum IV* [Brochure]. Detroit, MI: Author.

National Coaching Certification Council. (1978). *National coaching certification program.* Ottawa, Ontario: Author

National Council for Accreditation of Teacher Education (1992). NCATE board reaffirms standards. *NCATE Quality Teaching, 2*(1), 3.

National Council of Teachers of Mathematics. (1989, March). *Curriculum and evaluation standards for school mathematics.* Reston, VA: Author.

National Council on Education Standards and Testing. (1992). *Raising standards for American education.* Washington, DC: U.S. Government Printing Office.

National Dance-Exercise Instructor's Training Association. (1994). *Introducing advanced fitness certification* [Brochure]. Minneapolis, MN: Author.

National High School Athletic Coaches Association. (1990, March). Certification update. *National Coach.* Maitland, FL: Author.

National Recreation & Park Association, Michigan Recreation & Park Association. (1985, April). *Professional certification plan.*

National Safety Council. (1993). *National Safety Council first aid and CPR programs* [Brochure]. Boston, MA: First Aid and CPR Marketing, Jones and Bartlett Publishers.

National Strength and Conditioning Association. (1991). *1991 Practical principles of strength training and conditioning course.* Lincoln, NE: Author.

National Strength and Conditioning Association. (1985). *Position paper on anabolic drug use by athletes*. Lincoln, NE: Wright, J. E., & Stone, M. H.

National Strength and Conditioning Association. (1985). Position paper on prepubescent strength training. *National Strength and Conditioning Association Journal, 7*(4), 27-31.

Navar, N. (1981). A study of the professionalism of therapeutic recreation in the state of Michigan. *Therapeutic Recreation Journal, 15,* 50-56.

New York Public High School Athletic Association. (1990). *1990-92 Handbook.* Delmar, NY: Author.

NHSACA coaches code of ethics (1986, April-May-June). *National Coach.*

Noble, L., & Corbin, C. B. (1978). Professional preparation. *Journal of Physical Education and Recreation, 49*(2), 69-70.

NSCAA Coaching Academy. (1994, March/April). *Soccer Journal, 39*(2), 28.

....

O

Ocker, P. (1976, October). Coaching position statement. *The Michigan Journal*, 8-9.

O'Neil, J. (1991). Drive for national standards picking up steam. *Educational Research, 48*(50), 4-8.

....

P

Parkhouse, B. (1979). To win: What do you have to lose. *Journal of Physical Education and Recreation, 50,* 15-16.

Parks and Recreation Federation of Ontario (1983). *Are you certified?* North York, Ontario: Author.

Pearson, D. *Standards and assessment as tools of reform in American education.*

Peterson, J. A. (1991, December). How to compete for and keep the best employees. *Fitness Management, 7,* 30-33.

Pitts, E. H. (1994). Ensuring excellence without elitism. *Fitness Management, 10,* 6.
Pitts, E. H. (1994, May). Give me a break. *Fitness Management, 10,* 6.

Porter, A. C. (1989). External standards and good teaching: The pros and cons of telling teachers what to do. *Educational Evaluation and Policy Analysis, 11*(4), 343-356.

Professional Standards and Ethics Committee of the International Reading Association. (1978, May). *Guidelines for the professional preparation of reading teachers.* Newark, Delaware: Author.

Psychological testing of athletes. (1977, May). *Journal of Health, Physical Education, and Recreation, 48,* 30-32.

R

Research Consortium. (1985). Consortium position statement: The value of strength training for athletic success. *Research Consortium Newsletter, 8,* 4.

Reynolds, P. (1977, April). Games children play: Coaching makes a difference. *Selling Sporting Goods,* 43-46.

Roos, R. (1989). Certification for sports physicians gathers momentum. *The Physician and Sportsmedicine, 17*(2), 195-199.

Roos, R. (1987). Plan for accrediting fellowships worries sports orthopedists. *The Physician and Sportsmedicine, 15*(4), 151-160.

Ryan, A. J. (1981). Coaching certification: The real stone wall. *The Physician and Sportsmedicine, 9*(6), 35.

S

Sabock, R. J. (1981). Professional preparation for coaching. *Journal of Physical Education, Recreation & Dance, 52*(10), 10.

Sabock, R. J., & Chandler-Garvin, P. B. (1986). Coaching certification United States requirements. *JOPERD, 57,* 57-60.

Savastano, A. A. (1970). Rhode Island shows the way: In-service training for the prevention and treatment of athletic injuries. *Journal of Health, Physical Education, and Recreation, 41,* 54-58.

Sawyer, T. H., DuBois, P., Dalton, P., Houseworth, S., & Stover, D. (1991). Issues in interscholastic coaching certification. *NASPE News, 31,* 1, 6-7.

Schindler, B. (Ed.). (1994, August). *Standardization News, 22*(8).

Schmidt, L. (1985, Fall). Going out for the team. *Friendly Exchange,* 40-41.

Seefeldt, V. D. (1991). Coaching certification: An essential step for the revival of a faltering profession. *Journal of Physical Education, Recreation, and Dance, 63,* 29-30.

Seefeldt, V. D. (1979, March). *Certification of athletic coaches in Michigan's junior/middle and high schools, the fundamental question.* Unpublished manuscript presented to the committee on coaching certification of Michigan Association of Health, Physical Education and Recreation.

Seefeldt, V. D., & Milligan, M. J. (1992, September). Program for athletic coaches education (PACE) - Educating America's public & private school coaches. *Journal of Physical Education, Recreation, and Dance 64,* 46-49.

Selden, R. (1992, July). National standards and testing. *The State Board Connection, 12*(4), 2-5. National Association of State Boards of Education.

Sheets, N. L. (1971, June). Current status of certification of coaches in Maryland. *JOHPER, 42*(11), 11.

Siegel, D., & Newhof, C. (1992, January). Setting the standards for coaching curriculums: What should it take to be a coach? *Journal of Physical Education, Recreation and Dance, 63*, 60-63.

Siegel, D., & Newhof, C. (1992). What should it take to be a coach. *Journal of Physical Education, Recreation, and Dance, 63*, 60-63.

Sirotnik, K. A. (1985). Let's examine the profession, not the teachers. *Educational Leadership, 43*(3), 67-69.

Sisley, B. L. (1985). Off-the-street coaches: Methods for improving communication. *Journal of Physical Education, Recreation, and Dance, 56*, 63-66.

Sisley, B. (1984). Coaching specialization: The Oregon program. *The Physical Educator, 41*, 149-152.

Sizer, T. R., Rogers, B. (1993). Designing standards: Achieving. *Educational Leadership, 50*, 24-36.

Smith, B. J. (Ed.). (1993). *Journal of Heath Education, 24*(5).

Smith, J. A. & Jensen, S. (1985). Credentialing health educators: The issues. *Health Education, 16*, 28-29.

Smith, R. (1983). Keeping the quality in coaching or the quantity of coaches? *Sports Coach, 7*(1), 2-5.

Smith, R. A. (1983). Preludes to the NCAA: Early failures of faculty intercollegiate athletic control. *Research Quarterly for Exercise and Sport, 54*(4), 372-382.

Smith, R. E., Smoll, F. L., & Curtis, B. (1979). Coach efectiveness training: A cognitive-behavioral approach to enhancing relationship skills in youth sport coaches. *Journal of Sport Psychology, 1*, 59-75.

Smith, R. E., Smoll, F. L., & Hunt, E. B. (1972). *The effects of coaching behaviors on child athletes.* Seattle, WA: University of Washington, Departments of Psychology and Physical Education.

Spiker, J. C. (1979, September). Athletic trainer education. *JOPER, 50*, 72.

Staffo, D. F. (1991, October). Should administrators be specifically trained for positions in HPER-athletics? *JOPERD, 62*, 62-63, 78-79.

Staffo, D. F. (1978). Hints for selecting assistant coaches. *Coach and Athlete, 41*(1), 18;35-36.

Stier, W. F. (1983). Athletic administrators' expectations of coaches. *Journal of Physical Education, Recreation, and Dance, 54,* 57-59.

Successful promotion: Identify the problem before trying to solve it. (1985, March). *Athletic Business, 9,* 22-23.

Sweetser, E. R., Nelson, M. A., & Miranda, G. E. (1982). A county sports medicine committee. *The American Journal of SPorts Medicine, 10*(3), 184-187.

Sykes, G. (1989). National certification for teachers: A dialog. *NEA Today, 7,* 6-12.

T

Teacher certification. (1986). *ERIC Digest 11.*

Teicher, M. (1986). Certification for youth sports coaches a growing trend. *Presidents Council on Physical Fitness and Sports, 86*(2), 8.

Tenebaum, G., Singer, R. N., & Dishman, R. (1992). Physical activity and psychological benefits - International society of sport psychology position statement. *The Physician and Sportsmedicine, 20*(10), 179-184.

Tennessee Secondary School Athletic Association. (1992, August). *Summary Tennessee secondary school athletic association* (Draft dated 9/14/92). Hermitage, TN: Author.

Tennessee Secondary School Athletic Association. (1992, August). *Summary: Tennessee secondary school athletic association survey results, August 1992.* Hermitage, TN: Author.

Tharrett, S. J. (1994). ACSM certification meets '90's demands. *Fitness Management, 10,* 45-46.

Traulsen, J. (Ed.). (1992). Excellence or Conformity? The debate over national standards. *America's Agenda, 2*(3).

U

United States Olympic Comittee. (1983). US olympic committee establishes guidelines for sport psychology services. *Journal of Sport Psychology, 5,* 4-7.

United States Professional Tennis Registry's New Certification Testing Policy. (1994, November/December). *Tennis Pro, 12.*

United States Wrestling Federation. (1979, October). *USWF National Coaches Certification Program.*

University of Toledo. (1994). *Certified pool/spa operators course* [Brochure]. Toledo, OH: Author.

V

Valeriote, T. (1978). Coaching Certification. *Coaching Review, 1*(5), 29-31.

Valeriote, T. (1978). Who administers amateur sport in Canada? *Coaching Review, 1,* 40-44.

Varnes, J. W., & Crone, E. G. (1980). Teaching CPR to Florida's students. *Health Education, 11,* 21-23.

W

Walker, D. B. (1981). The Idaho model for certification. *JOHPERD, 52,* 64-65.

Watkins, B. T. (1993, September 22). 1,000 schoolteachers sign up for evaluations that would lead to national certification. *The Chronicle of Higher Education,* p. A19.

Weinberg, R. S. (1981, May). Why kids play or do not play organized sports. *The Physical Educator,* 71-76.

Welch, D. D. (1984). Teacher certification: There must be a better way. *The Chronicle of Higher Education.*

Weldon, G. (1978). Obtaining athletic training certification. *Coaching: Women's Athletics, 4*(5), 41 & 52.

White, N. (1990). Certification: ADs favor coaching program. *Athletic Director, 7,* 12-15, 52.

Winter, G. (1982). A child is not a little adult: An assessment of the response. *Sports Coach, 6*(2), 8-11.

Wishnietsky, D., & Felder, D. (1989). Coaching problems: Are suggested solutions effective. *Journal of Physical Education, Recreation, and Dancce, 60,* 69-72.

Wisniewski, F. J. (1981, Fall). Coaching compensation - Equal pay for equal work. *Michigan Journal of Health, Physical Education, Recreation, and Dance,* 16-19.

Woodman, L. (1993). Quality Coaching. *Sports Coach, 16*(4), 2.

Y

Young, J. R. (1994, August 3). Certifying eligibility. *The Chronicle of Higher Education,* A33.

Young, S. D. (1987). *The Rule of Experts.* Washington, DC: Cato Institute.

Z

Zimpher, N. L., & Loadman, W. E. (1986). A documentation and assessment system for student and program development. *ERIC Teacher Education Monograph No. 3.*

Zook, J. (1994, January 26). Education department revises controversial draft of accreditation regulations. *The Chronicle of Higher Education,* A36.